"Ray Comfort's teaching is right on. I

—**Joni Eareckson Tada**
Founder and President, Joni and Friends

"I have never heard the Gospel presented more powerfully, more correctly, or more clearly than when Kirk Cameron shared his message with us at Shadow Mountain Community Church."

—**Dr. David Jeremiah**
Senior Pastor, Shadow Mountain Community Church

"Ray Comfort is one of the most influential evangelists of our day. His humor and quick wit, combined with his potent teachings, give him the ability to reach the world with the Gospel like no other. I am blessed to call him a friend."

—**Chuck Missler**
Founder, Koinonia House

"[Ray Comfort]...a seasoned evangelist."

—**Franklin Graham**
President, Billy Graham Evangelistic Association

"Kirk Cameron gave one of the most sincere, simple, powerful statements of the Gospel I have ever heard."

—**John Piper**
Desiring God Ministries

"Ray Comfort brings us a word that cuts to the core of man's spiritual dilemma. As we pray for revival and wonder what God's waiting for, we need to seriously consider this message. To ignore it puts us in spiritual peril."

—**Terry Meeuwsen**
Cohost, *The 700 Club*

2

"[Kirk's teaching] puts a perspective on evangelism that will turn any congregation 180 degrees towards the lost...I highly recommend Kirk Cameron to those pastors who have a heart and desire to see their congregation catch the fire of evangelism through yet another vehicle to reach the world for which Christ died."

—Bob Coy
Senior Pastor, Calvary Chapel Ft. Lauderdale

"Ray Comfort is one of the freshest voices in Christian evangelism today."

—David E. Clippard
Director, Baptist General Convention of Oklahoma

3

RAY COMFORT & KIRK CAMERON

THE
WORLD'S GREATEST SERMONS & PREACHERS

W
WHITAKER
HOUSE

Editor's note: In the classic messages found in *The World's Greatest Sermons & Preachers*, the original Bible versions have been retained whenever possible. The texts of their messages, however, have been edited for the modern reader. Words, expressions, and sentence structure have been updated for clarity and readability.

THE WORLD'S GREATEST SERMONS & PREACHERS

(Previously titled *The World's Greatest Preachers*)

Living Waters
9818 Arkansas St.
Bellflower, CA 90706
www.livingwaters.com

ISBN: 978-1-64123-667-6
eBook ISBN: 978-1-64123-708-6
Printed in the United States of America
© 2003, 2021 by Ray Comfort and Kirk Cameron

Whitaker House
1030 Hunt Valley Circle
New Kensington, PA 15068
www.whitakerhouse.com

The Library of Congress has cataloged the original trade paperback edition as follows:
Comfort, Ray.
The world's greatest preachers / Ray Comfort and Kirk Cameron.
  p. cm.
ISBN 978-0-88368-942-4 (trade pbk. : alk. paper)
1. Sermons, English. I. Cameron, Kirk, 1970– II. Title.
BV4241.C66 2003
252'.3—dc22
                                                    2003014906

This book has been printed digitally and produced in a standard specification in order to ensure its continuing availability.

CONTENTS

PART TWO: OPEN-AIR PREACHING

FOREWORD
BY KIRK CAMERON

In these pages, we get to experience some of the greatest sermons ever preached by some of the most godly men who have ever lived. We are able to see not only how these great men of God presented the Gospel, but also how they used the "ten great cannons" of the divine Law to precede the Gospel message. They practiced principles that pulled down spiritual strongholds, leaving proud men humbled and even crying like babies, desperate for the salvation of their souls.

How did they do it? What made their sermons so amazingly powerful and effective? The answer is found in the principles and patterns they used to evangelize. While many today use man-made alternatives to biblical evangelism, these great preachers used the ultimate God-given spiritual weapon.

When reading Charles Spurgeon, it's easy to feel small. The man was nothing short of a genius. His grip on the English language was certainly phenomenal. His sanctified eloquence expressed the spirit of those who love God with a passion. Charles Spurgeon, John Wesley,

R. A. Torrey, and the others are *evangelistic* giants in the church's history, but the highly effective principles they used in their sermons were very simple and are attainable for us today. They employed biblical evangelism, and as these great preachers imitated the methods of Jesus—as well as the apostle Paul, Peter, and all the faithful preachers in Scripture—we can do the same. The common denominator of all these men was simply their love for God and the lost.

The first time I opened my mouth to share my faith, I was nervous. The first time I open-air preached, I was terrified. Irrational fear gripped my heart and clouded my mind as I thought of the ramifications of standing before a crowd of strangers, not knowing who might be listening as I voiced the very message that had caused the death of Jesus, Paul, Peter, and countless martyrs around the world. But to my surprise, I felt a deep sense of compassion for that crowd of unsaved people as I saw them struggling for answers to life's most important questions. I understood that they were sheep without a shepherd (Matthew 9:36), lost and destined for the lake of fire. They were without hope of redemption unless someone preached words of everlasting life to them that some might believe and be saved (Romans 10:9). The Holy Spirit compelled me, and I jumped up and began to speak without any thought of my own reputation. I had only an earnest compassion for them, and I began pleading with them to repent and turn back to the One who loved them and gave His life for them.

As Christians, our primary responsibility is to reach the lost. Just as Jesus left the comforts and pleasures of heaven to seek and save the lost, we, too, should be throwing open the doors of our sanctuaries, going out into the world, and bringing the life-giving message of the Gospel to a sick and dying generation.

The purpose of this book is to help equip you to be a faithful laborer for the Lord. Jesus said, *"The harvest truly is great, but the labourers are few: pray ye therefore the Lord of the harvest, that he would send forth labourers into his harvest"* (Luke 10:2). These sermons are not intended to overwhelm you with a sense of awe for the preachers themselves, but rather to motivate you to do what they did.

Where is the voice calling in the wilderness, *"Prepare ye the way of the Lord, make his paths straight"* (Matthew 3:3)? Where is today's Charles Spurgeon? Where are the true and faithful laborers, here, now, willing to abandon it all for the sake of saving precious souls? The harvest is still great, and, sadly, the laborers are still few. My prayer is that this book will stir you to offer yourself as a laborer.

After reading these sermons, you may want to learn more about how to effectively share your faith. You can do this through Living Waters' School of Biblical Evangelism. Visit us at www.livingwaters.com. We also have many other resources to help you, as well as a free e-mail news-letter to keep you up-to-date with what's happening in our ministry.

God bless you,
Kirk Cameron

PART ONE:

THE WORLD'S GREATEST SERMONS

John Wesley is a great inspiration.
As a young man consumed with a passion to reach the lost with the
Gospel, this former Anglican priest traveled thousands of miles on
horseback to preach the Gospel in small villages, large towns, and
wide-open fields filled with crowds of earnest listeners.
He actually preferred preaching the Gospel in the open air to
speaking within the walls of church buildings.
—Kirk

JOHN WESLEY

John Wesley was born June 17, 1703, the fifteenth child of Samuel, a former Nonconformist minister and rector at Epworth, England, and Susanna Wesley. His mother had eighteen other children and taught them daily from the Bible. When he was six, he was rescued from a house fire, causing his mother to call him "a brand plucked from the burning." (See Zechariah 3:2.) He would always remember this.

Wesley graduated from Oxford in 1724 and was ordained as an Anglican priest in the Church of England on September 22, 1728. In 1729, Wesley and his brother Charles founded a group called the Holy Club. They became known as Methodists, a derisive term for their emphasis on methodical study and devotion.

Under the influence of the Moravians, the group made a missionary journey to the Indians in the North American colony of Georgia from 1735–1737. The trip would greatly influence Wesley's life. He failed miserably due to his too-stern and terribly over-disciplined method. He wrote in his journal, "I went to America to convert the Indians; but oh, who shall convert me?"

Wesley struggled with this problem until one day in 1738 when he attended a service in which Martin Luther's "Preface to the Epistle to the Romans" was being read. Concerning the experience, Wesley wrote, "About a quarter before nine, while he was describing the change which God works in the heart through faith in Christ, I felt my heart strangely warmed. I felt I did trust in Christ:...An assurance was given me that He had taken away my sins, even mine, and saved me from the law of sin and death." Charles also experienced a religious awakening that convinced him salvation was possible through faith alone. From this point on, Wesley viewed his mission in life as one of proclaiming the good news of salvation by faith, which he did whenever a pulpit was offered to him.

In 1739 George Whitefield, who later became a great evangelical preacher in Great Britain and North America, persuaded Wesley to go to the unchurched masses. Wesley began to preach with new force and meaning and abandoned the church pulpit in favor of the outdoors. The response was so great—his first audience numbered about three thousand people—that he decided to preach wherever he could find an open ear, addressing as many as eight thousand at a time. But the more he preached in the fields, the more churches closed their pulpits to him.

Wesley believed that the entire world was his parish. His audience was made up of common laborers, such as miners, ironworkers, spinners, and weavers. He managed to complete a tour of England every year and made twenty visits to Scotland and Ireland. Traveling mostly on horseback, he covered an estimated two hundred fifty thousand miles and preached forty thousand sermons. In addition, he kept a detailed journal, wrote commentaries on Scripture, and edited classical works.

Wesley met with much opposition in his preaching. At times, he even faced angry mobs who objected to his claims of God's free offer of salvation. His meeting places were often looted and destroyed, and Wesley and his followers were subjected to frequent attacks.

Despite these problems, Wesley managed to visit prisons and poor-houses. He opened a free medical clinic, started the Stranger's Friend Society, and spoke out against slavery. All in all, John and his brother wrote several thousand hymns, including "Hark, the Herald Angels Sing" and "Christ the Lord Is Ris'n Today." Wesley worked until he was a feeble old man. He preached his last sermon just five days before he died on March 2, 1791. His last words were, "The best of all is, God is with us."

THE ORIGINAL, NATURE, PROPERTY, AND USE OF THE LAW

John Wesley
(Text from the 1872 edition)[1]

"Wherefore the law is holy,
and the commandment holy, and just, and good."
—Romans 7:12

There are few subjects within the whole compass of religion so little understood as the Law.[2] The reader of this epistle is usually told that, by the Law, Paul meant the Jewish Law, and so, understanding himself to have no concern with the Law, passes on without further thought about it. Indeed, some are not satisfied with this account; but observing that the epistle is directed to the Romans, they infer that the apostle alluded to the old Roman law in the beginning of this chapter. But as they have no more concern with this than with the ceremonial Law of Moses, they

---

1. If I [all footnotes are comments by Ray Comfort] may be so bold as to make this statement, John Wesley is incredibly methodical (he was the founder of the Methodists), and to some of us who are conditioned for quick answers and easy understanding (in these days of instant everything), Wesley's method may even seem a little laborious. But stay with him because he brings his thoughts to a wonderful climax.
2. We have capitalized the word *Law* throughout the book in order to distinguish it from civil law.

do not spend much thought on what they suppose is occasionally mentioned merely to illustrate another thing.

But a careful observer of the apostle's discourse will not be content with these light explications of it. And the more he weighs the words, the more convinced he will be that, by the Law mentioned in this chapter, Paul did not mean either the ancient law of Rome or the ceremonial Law of Moses. This will appear clear to all who attentively consider the theme of his discourse. He began the chapter, *"Know ye not, brethren, (for I speak to them that know the law,)"*—to those who had been instructed in the Law from their youth—*"that the law hath dominion over a man as long as he liveth?"* (Romans 7:1). (What law is discussed here? The law of Rome or the ceremonial Law? No, surely he meant the moral Law.[3]) To give a plain instance,

> *For the woman which hath an husband is bound by the* [moral] *law to her husband so long as he liveth; but if the husband be dead, she is loosed from the law of her husband. So then if, while her husband liveth, she be married to another man, she shall be called an adulteress: but if her husband be dead, she is free from that law; so that she is no adulteress, though she be married to another man.*
> (Romans 7:2–3)

From this particular instance the apostle proceeded to draw that general conclusion, by a plain inference of reason: *"Wherefore, my brethren ye also are become dead to the law"*—the whole Mosaic institution—*"by the body of Christ,"* which was offered for you and brings you under a new dispensation, namely, *"that ye should,"* without any blame, *"be married to another, even to him who is raised from the dead,"* and has thereby given proof of His authority to make the change, *"that we should bring forth fruit unto God"* (v. 4). And this we can do now, whereas before we could not: *"For when we were in the flesh"*—under the power of the flesh; that is, under the power of corrupt nature, which was necessarily

---

3. The Ten Commandments.

the case until we knew the power of Christ's resurrection—*"the motions of sins, which were by the law"*—which were shown and intensified by the Mosaic Law that had not yet been conquered—*"did work in our members"*—broke out in various ways—*"to bring forth fruit unto death"* (v. 5). *"But now we are delivered from the law"*—from that whole moral, as well as ceremonial, economy—*"that being dead wherein we were held"*—that entire institution being now dead and having no more authority over us than the husband, when dead, has over his wife—*"that we should serve"* Him who died for us and rose again *"in newness of spirit"*—in a new spiritual dispensation—*"and not in the oldness of the letter"*—not with a bare outward service, according to the letter of the Mosaic institution (v. 6).

The apostle, having gone thus far in proving that the Christian had set aside the Jewish dispensation and that the moral Law itself, though it could never pass away, yet stood on a different foundation from what it did before, then stopped to propose and answer an objection: *"What shall we say then? is the law sin?"* (Romans 7:7). So some might infer from a misapprehension of those words, *"the motions of sins, which were by the law"* (v 5). *"God forbid,"* said the apostle, that we should say so. No, the Law is an irreconcilable enemy to sin; for *"I had not known lust,"* or evil desire, to be sin, *"except the law had said, Thou shalt not covet"* (Romans 7:7). After opening this further, in the four following verses, he added this general conclusion, with regard especially to the moral Law, from which the preceding instance was taken: *"Wherefore the law is holy, and the commandment holy, and just, and good"* (v. 12).

In order to explain and enforce these deep words, so little regarded because they are so little understood, I will endeavor to show

1. the origin, or the source, of this Law,

2. the nature thereof,

3. the properties (that it is holy, and just, and good) and,

4. the uses of it.

THE SOURCE OF THE LAW

I will first endeavor to show the origin of the moral Law, often called "the" Law because of its prominence. Now this Law was not, as some may have possibly imagined, instituted as late as the time of Moses. Noah declared it to men long before that time, and Enoch before him. But we may trace its source higher still, even beyond the foundation of the world to that period, unknown indeed to men, but doubtless enrolled in the annals of eternity, when *"the morning stars"* first *"sang together"* (Job 38:7), being newly called into existence. It pleased the great Creator to make these, his firstborn sons, intelligent beings so that they might know the One who created them. For this purpose, He endued them with understanding to discern truth from falsehood, good from evil, and, as a necessary result of this—with liberty—a capacity of choosing the one and refusing the other. By this they were, likewise, enabled to offer Him a free and willing service, a service rewardable in itself as well as most acceptable to their gracious Master.

To employ all the faculties that He had given them, particularly their understanding and liberty, He gave the Law, a complete model of all truth, as far as it is intelligible to a finite being; and of all good, as far as angelic minds were capable of embracing it. It was also the design of their good Governor to provide a way for a continual increase of their happiness. Every instance of obedience to that Law would both add to the perfection of their nature and entitle them to a higher reward, which the righteous Judge would give in its season.

In like manner, God, in His appointed time, created a new order of intelligent beings. He had raised man from the dust of the earth, breathed into him the breath of life, and caused him to become a living soul, endued with power to choose good or evil. He gave to this free intelligent creature the same Law as to his firstborn children—not written, indeed, upon tables of stone or any corruptible substance, but engraved on man's heart by the finger of God, written in the inmost spirit both of men and of angels. By this, it might never be far off, never be hard to understand, but always at hand and always shining with clear light, even as the sun in the midst of heaven.

Such was the origin of the Law of God. With regard to man, the Law appeared in a manner to equal his nature; but with regard to the elder sons of God it shone in its full splendor *"before the mountains were brought forth, or ever thou hadst formed the earth and the world"* (Psalm 90:2). But it was not long before man rebelled against God, and by breaking this glorious Law, nearly erased it out of his heart. The eyes of his understanding were darkened in the same measure that his soul was *"alienated from the life of God"* (Ephesians 4:18). And yet God did not despise the work of His own hands, but, being reconciled to man through the Son of His love, He in some measure reinscribed the Law on the heart of His dark, sinful creature. Again, *"he hath showed thee, O man, what is good,"* although not as in the beginning, even *"to do justly, and to love mercy, and to walk humbly with thy God"* (Micah 6:8).

And this He showed, not only to our first parents but likewise to all their future offspring by that *"true Light which lighteneth every man that cometh into the world"* (John 1:9). But, notwithstanding this light, in process of time *"all flesh had corrupted his way upon the earth"* (Genesis 6:12) until He chose out of mankind a *"peculiar people"* (Deuteronomy 14:2; 1 Peter 2:9), to whom He gave a more perfect knowledge of His Law. Because they were slow of understanding, He wrote on two tables of stone the ten leaders of this Law, which He commanded the fathers to teach their children through all succeeding generations.

And so it is that the Law of God is now made known to those who do not know God. They hear with the hearing of the ear the things that were written long ago for our instruction. But this does not suffice: They cannot by this means comprehend the height, and depth, and length, and breadth of it. (See Ephesians 3:18.) God alone can reveal this by His Spirit. And so He does to all who truly believe, in consequence of that gracious promise made to all the Israel of God:

Behold, the days come, saith the LORD, *that I will make a new cov-*
enant with the house of Israel.… But this shall be the covenant that
I will make; I will put my law in their inward parts, and write it in
their hearts; and will be their God, and they shall be my people.

(Jeremiah 31:31, 33)

THE NATURE OF THE LAW

The nature of this Law, which was originally given to angels in heaven and man in Paradise, and which God has so mercifully promised to write afresh in the hearts of all true believers, is the second thing I propose to show. In order to do so, I would first observe that although the "Law" and the "commandment" are sometimes differently taken (the commandment meaning a part of the Law), yet in the text they are used as equivalent terms, implying one and the same thing. But we cannot understand here, either by one or the other, the ceremonial Law. It is not the ceremonial Law of which the apostle said, *"I had not known sin, but by the law"* (Romans 7:7)—this is too plain to need a proof. Neither was it the ceremonial Law that said, in the words immediately following, *"Thou shalt not covet"* (v. 7). Therefore, the ceremonial Law has no place in the present question.

Neither can we interpret the Law mentioned in the text as the Mosaic dispensation. It is true the word is sometimes so understood, as when the apostle said, speaking to the Galatians, *"The covenant… that was confirmed before"*—namely, with Abraham, the father of the faithful—*"the law"*—that is the Mosaic dispensation—*"which was four hundred and thirty years after, cannot disannul"* (Galatians 3:17). But it cannot be so understood in the text, for the apostle never bestowed commendations as high as these upon that imperfect and shadowy dispensation. He nowhere affirmed the Mosaic to be a spiritual law, nor did he say that it is holy, just, and good. Neither is it true that God will write that Law in the hearts of those whose iniquities He remembers no more. It remains that *"the law,"* notably so termed, is no other than the moral Law.

Now, this Law is an incorruptible picture of the High and Holy One who inhabits eternity. It is He, in His essence no man has seen or can see, made visible to men and angels. It is the face of God unveiled. God manifested Himself to His creatures as they are able to bear it, manifested to give and not to destroy life—so that they may see God and live. It is the heart of God disclosed to man. Yes, in some sense we may apply to this Law what the apostle said of His Son: It is *apaugasma doxa charakter hupostasis phero*—the streaming forth or out-beaming of His glory, *"the express image of His person"* (Hebrews 1:3).

"If virtue," said an ancient heathen, "could assume a shape that we could behold with our eyes, what wonderful love would she excite in us!" If virtue could do this! It is done already. The Law of God is all virtues in one, in such a shape that all those whose eyes God has enlightened can behold openly. What is the Law but divine virtue and wisdom assuming a visible form? What is it but the original ideas of truth and good, which were lodged in the uncreated mind from eternity, now drawn forth and clothed in order to appear to our limited human understanding?

If we survey the Law of God from another point of view, it is supreme unchangeable reason. It is unalterable righteousness, the ever-lasting fitness of all things that are or ever were created. I am aware of what shortness, and even impropriety, there is in these and all other human expressions when we endeavor by these faint pictures to shadow out the deep things of God. Nevertheless, we have no better—indeed, no other—way during this, our infant state of existence. As we now *"know"* but *"in part,"* so we are constrained to *"prophesy"*—that is, to speak of the things of God—*"in part,"* also (1 Corinthians 13:9). *"We cannot order our speech by reason of darkness"* (Job 37:19) while we are in this house of clay. While I am *"a child"* I must speak *"as a child."* But I will soon *"put away childish things"* (1 Corinthians 13:11), for *"when that which is perfect is come, then that which is in part shall be done away"* (v. 10).

But to return: The Law of God (speaking after the manner of men) is a copy of the eternal mind, a transcript of the divine nature. Yes, it is the fairest offspring of the everlasting Father, the brightest outflow of His essential wisdom, the visible beauty of the Most High. It is the delight and wonder of cherubim and seraphim and all the company of heaven, and the glory and joy of every wise believer, every well-instructed child of God upon the earth.

PROPERTIES OF THE LAW

Such is the nature of the ever blessed Law of God. In the third place I propose to show the properties of the Law. Not all, for that would exceed the wisdom of an angel, but those that are mentioned in the text. There are three properties: It is holy, just, and good. And, first, the Law is holy.

In this expression the apostle did not appear to speak of its effects, but rather of its nature. As James, speaking of the same thing under another name, said, *"The wisdom that is from above* [which is no other than this Law, written in our heart] *is first pure"* (James 3:17)—*hagnos*—meaning chaste, spotless; eternally and essentially *holy*. And, consequently, when it is transcribed into the life, as well as the soul, it is (as the same apostle termed it) *katharos threskeia amiantos*—*"pure religion and undefiled"* (James 1:27), or the pure, clean, unpolluted worship of God.

The Law is indeed, in the highest degree, pure, chaste, clean, and holy. Otherwise it could not be the immediate offspring, and much less the express resemblance, of God, who is essential holiness. It is pure from all sin, clean and unspotted from any touch of evil. It is a chaste virgin, incapable of any defilement, of any interaction with that which is unclean or unholy. It has no fellowship with sin of any kind. For *"what communion hath light with darkness"* (2 Corinthians 6:14)? As sin is, in its very nature, enmity to God, so His Law is enmity to sin.

Therefore, the apostle rejected with such abhorrence the blasphemous supposition that the Law of God is either sin itself or the cause of sin. God forbid that we would suppose the Law is the *cause* of sin, because it is the *discoverer* of sin. It detects the hidden things of darkness and drags them out into open day. It is true, by this means (as the apostle observed) *"sin…might appear* [to be] *sin"* (Romans 7:13). All sin's disguises are torn away and it appears in its native deformity. It is true, likewise, that *"sin by the commandment becomes exceeding sinful"* (v. 13). Being now committed against light and knowledge, being stripped even of the poor plea of ignorance, it loses its excuse, as well as disguise, and becomes far more odious both to God and man. Yes, *"sin* [works] *death…by that which is good"* (Romans 7:13), which in itself is pure and holy. When it is dragged out to light, sin rages even more. When it is restrained, it bursts out with greater violence. Thus the apostle (speaking as one who was convinced of sin, but not yet delivered from it) said, *"Sin, taking occasion by the commandment"* detecting and endeavoring to restrain it, disdained the restraint, and so much the more *"wrought in me all manner of concupiscence"* (Romans 7:8), all manner of foolish and hurtful desire, which that commandment sought to restrain. Thus, *"when the commandment came, sin revived"* (Romans 7:9); it fretted and raged the more. But this is no stain on the commandment. Though it is abused, it cannot be defiled. This proves only that the heart of man is *"desperately wicked"* (Jeremiah 17:9). But *"the Law"* of God *"is holy"* still.

Second, the Law is just. It renders to all their due. It prescribes exactly what is right, precisely what ought to be done, said, or thought—both with regard to the Author of our being, with regard to ourselves, and with regard to every creature that He has made. It is adapted, in all respects, to the nature of things, of the whole universe and every individual. It is suited to all the circumstances of each, and to all their mutual relations, whether such as have existed from the beginning, or such as commenced in any following period. It is exactly agreeable to the fitnesses of things, whether essential or nonessential. It clashes with none of these in any degree. Nor is it ever unconnected with them. If the word is taken in that sense, there is nothing arbitrary in the Law of God. Although still the whole and every part thereof is totally dependent upon His will, so that "Your will be done" is the supreme universal Law both in earth and heaven.

"But is the will of God the cause of His Law? Is His will the original of right and wrong? Is a thing, therefore, right because God wills it? Or does He will it because it is right?"

I fear this celebrated question is more curious than useful. And perhaps in the manner it is usually treated, it does not so well exist with the regard that is due from a creature to the Creator and Governor of all things. It is hardly decent for man to call the supreme God to give an account to him. Nevertheless, with awe and reverence we may speak a little. The Lord pardon us if we speak amiss!

It seems, then, that the whole difficulty arises from considering God's will as distinct from God; otherwise it vanishes away. For none can doubt that God is the cause of the Law of God. The will of God is God Himself. It is God as we consider Him willing this or that. Consequently, to say that the will of God, or that God Himself, is the cause of the Law, is one and the same thing.

Again, if the Law, the immutable rule of right and wrong, depends upon the nature and fitness of things and on their essential relation to each other (I do not say their eternal relations because the eternal relation of things existing in time is little less than a contradiction). If I say this depends on the nature and relations of things, then it must depend on God or the will of God, because those things themselves, with all their relations, are the works of His hands. By His will, "*for* [His] *pleasure*" alone, they all "*are and were created*" (Revelation 4:11).

And yet it may be granted (which is probably all that a considerate person would contend for) that in every particular case, God wills this or that (suppose, that men should honor their parents) because it is right and agreeable concerning their relationship.

The Law, then, is right and just concerning all things. And it is good as well as just. This we may easily infer from the fountain from which it flowed. For what was this, but the goodness of God? What but goodness alone inclined Him to impart that divine copy of Himself to the holy angels? To what else can we impute His bestowing upon man the same transcript of His own nature? And what, except tender love, constrained Him afresh to manifest His will to fallen man—either to Adam or any of his seed, who, like him, were *"come short of the glory of God"* (Romans 3:23)? Was it not mere love that moved Him to publish His Law after the understandings of men were darkened? And to send His prophets to declare that Law to the blind, thoughtless children of men? Doubtless it was His goodness that raised up Enoch and Noah to be preachers of righteousness; that caused Abraham, His friend, and Isaac and Jacob, to bear witness to His truth. It was His goodness alone that, when *"a day of darkness and of gloominess, a day of clouds and of thick darkness"* had covered the earth (Joel 2:2), gave a written Law to Moses and, through Moses, to the nation whom He had chosen. It was love that explained these living oracles by David and all the prophets that followed, until, when the fullness of time was come, He sent His only begotten Son *"not…to destroy [the Law]…but to fulfill"* (Matthew 5:17) and confirm every jot and tittle thereof (v. 18); until, having written it in the hearts of all His children, and put all His enemies under His feet, He will deliver His kingdom that was entrusted to Him back to the Father, *"that God may be all in all"* (1 Corinthians 15:28).

And this Law, which the goodness of God gave at first and has preserved through all ages, is like the fountain from whence it springs, full of goodness and benignity. It is mild and kind. It is, as the psalmist expressed it, *"sweeter also than honey and the honeycomb"* (Psalm 19:10). It is winning and amiable. It includes *"whatsoever things are lovely or of good report; if there be any virtue, if there be any praise"* (Philippians

4:8) before God and His holy angels, they are all comprised in this—in which all the treasures of the divine wisdom and knowledge and love are hidden.

And it is good in its effects, as well as in its nature. As the tree is, so are its fruits. The fruits of the Law of God written in the heart are *"righteousness...peace...and assurance for ever"* (Isaiah 32:17). Or rather, the Law itself is righteousness, filling the soul with a peace that passes all understanding and causing us to rejoice evermore in the testimony of a good conscience toward God. It is so, too, properly a pledge as *"the earnest of our inheritance"* (Ephesians 1:14), being a part of the purchased possession. It is God made manifest in our flesh and bringing with Him eternal life, assuring us by that pure and perfect love that we are *"sealed unto the day of redemption"* (Ephesians 4:30), that He will *"spare us as a man spares His own son that serves him"* (see Malachi 3:17), *"in that day when [He] make[s] up [His] jewels"* (verse 17), and that there remains for us *"a crown of glory that fadeth not away"* (1 Peter 5:4).

THE USES OF THE LAW

Fourth, to show the uses of the Law remains. Without question, the first use of it is to convince the world of sin. This is, indeed, the distinctive work of the Holy Spirit, who can work it without any means at all or by whatever means it pleases Him, however unlikely in themselves, or even insufficient, to produce such an effect. And accordingly, there are some whose hearts have been broken in pieces in a moment, either in sickness or in health, without any visible cause or any outward means whatever, and others who have been awakened to a sense of the "wrath of God" abiding on them by hearing that *"God was in Christ, reconciling the world unto himself"* (2 Corinthians 5:19). But it is the ordinary method of the Spirit of God to convict sinners by the Law. It is this that, being set home on the conscience, generally breaks the rocks in pieces. It is more especially this part of the Word of God that is *zao* and *energes*—*"quick, and powerful"*—full of life and energy and *"sharper than any twoedged sword*" (Hebrews 4:12). This, in the hand of God and of those whom He has sent, pierces through the folds of a deceitful heart and divides asunder even the soul and the spirit, yes, as it were, the very "*joints and marrow*" (v. 12). By this the sinner discovers himself. All his fig leaves are torn away and he sees that he is "*wretched, and miserable, and poor, and blind, and naked*" (Revelation 3:17). The Law flashes conviction on every side. He feels himself a mere sinner. He has nothing to pay. His "*mouth* [is] *stopped*," and he stands "*guilty before God*" (Romans 3:19).

To slay the sinner is then the first use of the Law—to destroy the life and strength he trusts in and convince him that he is dead while he lives, not only under the sentence of death, but actually dead unto God, void of all spiritual life, "*dead in trespasses and sins*" (Ephesians 2:1).

The second use of it is to bring him to life and to Christ so that he may live. In performing both these offices, the Law acts the part of a severe schoolmaster. It drives us by force, rather than drawing us by love. And yet love is the spring of all.[4] By this painful means, the spirit of love tears away our confidence in the flesh, which leaves us no broken reed to trust (see Isaiah 36:6) and so constrains the sinner, stripped of everything, to cry out in the bitterness of his soul or groan in the depth of his heart, "I give up every plea beside—Lord, I am damn'd; but Thou hast died."

The third use of the Law is to keep us alive. It is the grand means the blessed Spirit uses to prepare the believer for larger revelations about the life of God.

I am afraid this great and important truth is little understood, not only by the world, but even by many whom God has taken out of the world, who are real children of God by faith. Many of these believe, as an unquestioned truth, that when we come to Christ, we are done with the Law, and that, in this sense, "*Christ is the end of the law…to every one*

---

4. This is an absolutely essential point to understand since many consider the use of the Law in evangelism to be just the opposite.

that believeth" (Romans 10:4). *"Christ is the end of the law for righteousness"* (v. 4)—for justification—*"to every one that believeth."* In Christ, the Law is at an end. It justifies none, but only brings them to Christ, who is also, in another respect, the end or aim of the Law—the point at which it continually aims. But when the Law has brought us to Him, it has yet a further office—namely, to keep us with Him. For it is continually inspiring all believers, the more they see of its height, depth, length, and breadth, to exhort one another so much more:

> Closer and closer let us cleave
>
> To His beloved embrace;
>
> Expect His fullness to receive,
>
> And grace to answer grace.

Allowing then that every believer is done with the Law, meaning the Jewish ceremonial Law or the entire Mosaic dispensation (for these Christ has taken out of the way). Yes, assenting that we are done with the moral Law as a means of procuring our justification. For we are *"justified freely by his grace through the redemption that is in Christ Jesus"* (Romans 3:24).

Yet, in another sense, we are not done with this Law. For it is still of unspeakable use, first, in convincing us of the sin that yet remains both in our hearts and lives, and thereby keeping us close to Christ so that His blood may cleanse us every moment. Second, in deriving strength from our Head into His living members, by which He empowers them to do what His Law commands. And, third, in confirming our hope of whatsoever it commands and we have not yet attained—of receiving grace upon grace, until we are in actual possession of the fullness of His promises.

How clearly does this agree with the experience of every true believer! While he cries out, "Oh, what love have I to Your law! All day long I study it," he sees daily, in that divine mirror, more and more of his own sinfulness. He sees more and more clearly that he is still a sinner in all things—that neither his heart nor his ways are right before God and that every moment sends him to Christ. This shows him the meaning of what is written: *"Thou shalt make a plate of pure gold, and grave upon it...*HOLINESS TO THE LORD.... *And it shall be upon Aaron's forehead* [the example of our great High Priest] *that Aaron may bear the iniquity of the holy things, which the children of Israel shall hallow in all their holy gifts* [so far are our prayers or holy things from atoning for the rest of our sin!]; *and it shall be always upon his forehead, that they may be accepted before the* LORD" (Exodus 28:36, 38).

To explain this by a single instance: The Law says, *"Thou shalt not kill"* (Exodus 20:13), and by this (as our Lord taught) forbids not only outward acts, but also every unkind word or thought. Now, the more I look into this perfect Law, the more I feel how far I come short of it, and the more I feel this, the more I feel my need of His blood to atone for all my sin and of His Spirit to purify my heart and make me *"perfect and entire, wanting nothing"* (James 1:4).

Therefore, I cannot spare the Law one moment, no more than I can spare Christ. I now want the Law as much to keep me near Christ as I ever wanted it to bring me to Him. Otherwise, this *"evil heart of unbelief"* would immediately *"[depart] from the living God"* (Hebrews 3:12). Indeed, each is continually sending me to the other—the Law to Christ, and Christ to the Law.[5] On the one hand, the height and depth of the Law constrain me to fly to the love of God in Christ; on the other, the love of God in Christ endears the Law to me above gold or precious stones. I know every part of it is a gracious promise that my Lord will fulfill in its season.

---

5. This is such a wonderful point. It is no accident that we at Living Waters have entitled our teaching that exposes the use of the Law "Hell's Best Kept Secret." (Listen to this teaching online at www.livingwaters.com.) The enemy hates the Law because it not only equips the Christian with the most powerful evangelistic weapon, but it also has the power to produce holiness in the life of the believer. Knowledge of the spiritual nature of the Law keeps us in a place of humility, at the foot of the Cross. That is not only a place of safety, but it is also the secret of power with God. (See Romans 1:4.)

Who are you, then, O man, who "judges the Law, and speaks evil of the Law" (see James 4:11)—who ranks the Law with sin, Satan, and death and sends them all to hell together? The apostle James esteemed judging or "speaking evil of the Law" a piece of wickedness so enormous that he did not know how to increase the guilt of judging our fellow Christians more than by showing it included this. "So now," said he, *"thou art not a doer of the law, but a judge"* (v. 11). A judge of that which God has ordained to judge in you. So you have set up yourself in the judgment seat of Christ and cast down the rule by which He will judge the world! See what an advantage Satan has gained over you. For the time to come, never think or speak lightly of—much less dress up as a scarecrow—this blessed instrument of the grace of God. Yes, love and value it for the sake of Him from whom it came and of Him to whom it leads. Let it be your glory and joy, next to the Cross of Christ. Declare its praise, and make it honorable before all men.

And if you are thoroughly convinced that it is the offspring of God, that it is the copy of all His inimitable perfections, and that it is *"holy, and just, and good"* (Romans 7:12), but especially to those who believe, then, instead of casting it away as a polluted thing, see that you cleave to it more and more. Never let the Law of mercy and truth, of love to God and man, of lowliness, meekness, and purity, forsake you. *"Bind them about thy neck; write them upon the table of thine heart"* (Proverbs 3:3). Keep close to the Law if you will keep close to Christ; hold it fast; do not let it go. Let this continually lead you to the atoning blood, continually confirm your hope until all the "righteousness of the Law is fulfilled in you" (see Romans 8:4), and you are *"filled with all the fulness of God"* (Ephesians 3:19).

And if your Lord has already fulfilled His word, if He has already "written His Law in your heart," then *"stand fast...in the liberty wherewith Christ hath made us free"* (Galatians 5:1). You are not only made free from Jewish ceremonies, from the guilt of sin, and the fear of hell (these are so far from being the whole that they are the least and lowest part of Christian liberty), but what is infinitely more, from the power of sin, from serving the devil, from offending God. Oh, stand fast in this liberty, in comparison of which all the rest is not even worthy to be named! Stand fast in loving God with all your heart, and serving Him with all your strength! This is perfect freedom. Thus, to keep His Law, and to walk in all His commandments blameless, *be not entangled again with the yoke of bondage*" (Galatians 5:1). I do not mean of Jewish bondage, nor yet of bondage to the fear of hell. These, I trust, are far from you. But beware of being entangled again with the yoke of sin, of any inward or outward transgression of the Law. Abhor sin far more than death or hell. Abhor sin itself far more than the punishment of it. Beware of the bondage of pride, of desire, of anger, of every evil temper, word, or work. "Look to Jesus" (see Hebrews 12:2), and in order to do so look more and more into the perfect Law—"*the law of liberty*" (James 1:25)—and "*continueth therein*" (v. 25) so you will daily "*grow in grace, and in the knowledge of our Lord and Saviour Jesus Christ*" (2 Peter 3:18).

If ever there was a preacher whose words epitomized "sanctified eloquence," it was Charles Spurgeon.
From the time he was very young, he spoke with wisdom, spiritual maturity, and effectiveness, which were obviously inspired by the Master. His doctrine was pure, his love for God was deep, and his concern for the lost was infectious.
I can't read something from Spurgeon without feeling as though I have indeed received a word from one of the world's greatest preachers.
—Kirk

CHARLES SPURGEON

Charles Haddon Spurgeon was born on June 19, 1834, at Kelvedon, Essex, England, the firstborn of eight surviving children. His parents were committed Christians, and his father was a preacher. After Spurgeon was converted in 1850 at the age of fifteen, he began helping the poor and handing out tracts. He was soon known as "The Boy Preacher."

His next six years were eventful. He preached his first sermon at the age of sixteen to a group of farm laborers and their wives in a thatched cottage in Teversham, England. At age eighteen, he became the pastor of Waterbeach Baptist Chapel, preaching in a barn. Spurgeon preached over six hundred times before he reached the age of twenty. Behind this success was a man who rose early every morning to pray and read the Bible. For two years, he maintained the habit, and the fruits were easy to see. More and more people wanted to hear him speak.

By 1854 he was well known and was invited to become the pastor of New Park Street Chapel in London. In 1856 Spurgeon married

Susannah Thompson; they had twin sons, both of whom later entered the ministry.

Spurgeon's compelling sermons and lively preaching style drew multitudes of people, and many came to Christ. Soon, the crowds had grown so large that they blocked the narrow streets near the church. Services eventually had to be held in rented halls, and he often preached to congregations of more than ten thousand. The Metropolitan Tabernacle was built in 1861 to accommodate for the large numbers of people. Spurgeon became so well known that the cabbies used to talk of taking their fares "over the river to Charlie."

Spurgeon liked to prepare his sermons on Saturday evenings and Sunday afternoons when he would jot down his thoughts in shorthand. On Mondays, he would revise them and write them out in full so they could be printed and published on Thursdays. He published over two thousand sermons, which were so popular that they literally sold by the ton. At one point, his sermons sold twenty-five thousand copies each week. An 1870 edition of the English magazine *Vanity Fair* called him an "original and powerful preacher...honest, resolute, sincere; lively, entertaining." He appealed constantly to his hearers to move on in the Christian faith, to allow the Lord to minister to them individually, and to be used by God to win the lost to Christ. His sermons were scripturally inspiring and often filled with flashes of spontaneous and delightful humor. The prime minister of England, members of the royal family, and Florence Nightingale, among others, went to hear him preach. Spurgeon preached to an estimated ten million people throughout his life. Not surprisingly, he is called "The Prince of Preachers."

In addition to his powerful preaching, Spurgeon founded and supported charitable outreaches, including educational institutions. His pastors' college, which still exists today, taught nearly nine hundred students during Spurgeon's time. He also founded the famous Stockwell Orphanage.

In his later years, Spurgeon often publicly disagreed with the emergence of modern biblical criticism that led the believer away from a total dependence on the Word of God. He was called "The Last of the Puritans" because, although he lived one hundred years after the Puritans, he expressed their theology accurately. All he wanted to do in his preaching life, he said, was present Jesus Christ and base all his teachings on the Word of God.

Charles Spurgeon died in Mentone, France in 1892, leaving a legacy of writings to the believer who seeks to know the Lord Jesus more fully. An editor of Spurgeon's day said that "[his life will] continue to be studied with growing interest and wonder, and will ultimately be accepted as incomparably the greatest contribution to the literature of experimental Christianity that has been made in this century."

THE USES OF THE LAW

C. H. Spurgeon
A Sermon Delivered on Sabbath Morning, April 19, 1857, at
the Music Hall, Royal Surrey Gardens

"Wherefore then serveth the law?"
—Galatians 3:19

The apostle, by a highly ingenious and powerful argument, proved that the Law was never intended by God for the justification and salvation of man. He declared that God made a covenant of grace with Abraham long before the Law was given to Moses on Mount Sinai. In addition, Abraham was not present at Mount Sinai and, therefore, there could have been no alteration of the covenant made there without his consent. Moreover, Abraham's consent was never asked as to any alteration of the covenant, without which the covenant could not have been lawfully changed, and, besides that, the covenant stands fast and firm, since it was made to Abraham's seed, as well as to Abraham himself.

And this I say, that the covenant, that was confirmed before of God in Christ, the law, which was four hundred and thirty years after, cannot disannul, that it should make the promise of none effect. For if the inheritance be of the law, it is no more of promise: but God gave it to Abraham by promise. (Galatians 3:17–18)

Therefore, no inheritance and no salvation can ever be obtained by the Law. Ignorance leads men to become extremists. Generally, when men believe one truth, they carry it so far that they deny another. Very frequently, the assertion of a cardinal truth leads men to generalize on other particulars, and so they make falsehoods out of truth. One may object, "Paul said that the Law cannot justify. Surely then the Law is good for nothing at all; *'wherefore then serveth the Law?'* If it will not save a man, what good is it? If it can never take a man to heaven, why was it written? Is it not a useless thing?"[6] The apostle might have replied to his opponent with a sneer; he must have said to him, "O fool, and slow of heart to understand: Is a thing utterly useless because it is not intended for every purpose in the world? Will you say that, because iron cannot be eaten, therefore, iron is not useful? And because gold cannot be food for man, will you, therefore, cast gold away and call it worthless dross? Yet on your foolish supposition you must do so. For, because I have said the Law cannot save, you have foolishly asked me what the use of it is, and you foolishly suppose God's Law is good for nothing and can be of no value whatever."

This objection is, generally, brought forward by two sorts of people. First, by mere quibblers who do not like the Gospel and wish to pick all sorts of holes in it. They can tell us what they do not believe, but they do not tell us what they do believe. They would fight with everybody's doctrines and sentiments, but they would be at a loss if they were asked to sit down and write their own opinions. They do not seem to have gotten much further than the genius of the monkey, which can pull everything to pieces but can put nothing together. Then, on the other hand, there is the Antinomian, who says, "Yes, I know I am saved by grace alone," and then breaks the Law. He says it is not binding on him, even as common sense, and asks, "What purpose does the Law serve?" throwing it out like an old piece of furniture fit only for the fire because it is not adapted to save his soul. Why, a thing may have many uses, though it does fulfill others. It is true that the Law cannot save; yet it is equally true that the

6. Ask most Christians why God gave His Law, and they will speak of it with disdain.

Law is one of the highest works of God, is deserving of all reverence, and is extremely useful when applied by God to the purposes for which it was intended.

Yet, pardon me, my friends, if I just observe that this is a very natural question, too. If you read the doctrine of the apostle Paul, you find him declaring that the Law condemns all mankind. Now, just let us for one single moment take a bird's-eye view of the works of the Law in this world. Behold, I see the Law given upon Mount Sinai. The very hill quakes with fear. Lightnings and thunders are the attendants of those dreadful syllables that make the hearts of Israel melt. Sinai seemed completely covered in smoke. The Lord came from Paran, and the Holy One from Mount Sinai: *"He came with ten thousands of saints"* (Deuteronomy 33:2). Out of His mouth came a fiery Law for them. It was a dreadful Law, even when it was given, and, since then, an awful lava of vengeance has run down from Mount Sinai that would have deluged, destroyed, burned, and consumed the whole human race if Jesus Christ had not stemmed its awful torrent and bidden its waves of fire to be still. If you could see the world without Christ in it, simply under the Law, you would see a world in ruins, a world with God's black seal put upon it, stamped and sealed for condemnation. You would see men who, if they knew their condition, would have their hands over their faces and be groaning all their days. You would see men and women condemned, lost, and ruined. In the uttermost regions you would see the pit that is dug for the wicked, into which the whole earth would have been cast if the Law had its way apart from the Gospel of Jesus Christ, our Redeemer.

Yes, beloved, the Law is a great deluge, which would have drowned the world with worse than the water of Noah's flood. It is a great fire, which would have burned the earth with a destruction worse than that which fell on Sodom. It is a stern angel with a sword, thirsty for blood and winged to slay. It is a great destroyer sweeping down the nations. It is the great messenger of God's vengeance sent into the world. Apart from the Gospel of Jesus Christ, the Law is nothing but the condemning voice of God thundering against mankind. "What purpose does the Law serve?" seems a very natural question. Can the Law be of any benefit to man? Can that Judge who puts on a black cap and condemns us all, this Lord Chief Justice Law, can he help in salvation? Yes, he did; and you will see how he does it, if God helps me while I preach. "What purpose does the Law serve?"

TO SHOW MAN HIS GUILT

The first use of the Law is *to manifest man's guilt to him.* When God intends to save a man, the first thing He does with him is to send the Law to him, to show him how guilty, how vile, how ruined he is, and how dangerous a position he is in. You see that man lying there on the edge of the precipice; he is sound asleep and just on the perilous verge of the cliff. One single movement, and he will roll over and be broken in pieces on the jagged rocks beneath, and nothing more will be heard from him. How is he to be saved? What shall be done for him? This is our position—we, too, are lying on the brink of ruin, but we do not know it. When God begins to save us from such an imminent danger, He sends His Law, which wakes us up with a stout kick and makes us open our eyes. We look down on our terrible danger and discover our miseries; then we are in the right position to cry out for salvation, and our salvation comes to us. The Law acts with man just as the physician does when he takes the film from the eyes of the blind. Self-righteous men are blind men, though they think themselves good and excellent. The Law takes that film away and lets them discover how vile they are and how utterly ruined and condemned they are if they are to abide under the sentence of the Law.

Instead of treating this doctrinally, however, I will treat it practically, in order to hit home with each of your consciences. Friend, does the Law of God not convince you of sin this morning? Under the hand of God's Spirit, do you not feel that you have been guilty, that you deserve to be lost, and that you have incurred the fierce anger of God? Look here, have you not broken the Ten Commandments? Have you not broken them even to the letter? Who is there among us who has always honored his father and mother? Who is there among us who has always spoken the truth? Have we not sometimes borne false witness against our neighbor? Is there one person here who has not made himself another god and loved himself or his business or his friends more than he has loved Jehovah, the God of the whole earth? Which of you has not coveted your neighbor's house or his manservant or his ox or his ass? (See Exodus 20:17.)

We are all guilty with regard to every letter of the Law. We have all of us transgressed the commandments. And if we really understood these commandments and felt that they condemned us, they would show us our danger, and so lead us to fly to Christ. But, my hearers, does this Law not condemn you, because even if you would say you have not broken the letter of it, yet you have violated the spirit of it. Though you have never killed, we are told that he who is angry with his brother is a murderer. As a man said once, "Sir, I thought I had never killed—I was innocent there; but when I heard that he who hates his brother is a murderer, then I cried guilty, for I have killed twenty men before breakfast very often, for I have been angry with many of them very often." This Law does not mean only what it says in words, but it has deep things hidden in its bowels. It says, *"Thou shalt not commit adultery"* (Exodus 20:14), but it means, as Jesus said, *"Whosoever looketh on a woman to lust after her hath committed adultery with her already in his heart"* (Matthew 5:28). When it says, *"Thou shalt not take the name of the LORD thy God in vain"* (Exodus 20:7), it means that we should reverence God in every place and have His fear before our eyes, and we should always pay respect unto His ordinances and walk in His fear and love. Yes, my friends, surely there is not one here so foolhardy in self-righteousness as to say, "I am innocent." The spirit of the Law condemns us. And this is its useful property; it humbles us, makes us know we are guilty, and so we are led to receive the Savior.

Mark this, my dear hearers, *one breach of this Law is enough to condemn us forever.* He who breaks the Law in one point is guilty of the whole. (See James 2:10.) The Law demands that we obey every command. If one of them is broken, all of them are injured. It is like a vase of surpassing workmanship: In order to destroy it, you do not need to shiver it to atoms. If you make the smallest fracture in it, you have destroyed its perfection. It is a perfect Law[7] that we are commanded to obey and to obey perfectly. Just one breach in it and, though we are ever so innocent, we can hope for nothing from the Law except the voice, "You are condemned, you are condemned, you are condemned." Under this aspect of the matter, should the Law not strip many of us of all our boasting? Who is there who will rise in his place and say, "Lord, *'I thank thee, that I am not as other men are'* (Luke 18:11)"? Surely there cannot be one among you who can go home and say, "I have tithed mint and cummin (see Matthew 23:23); I have kept all the commandments from my youth (see Matthew 19:20)"? No, if this Law is brought home to the conscience and the heart, we will stand with the publican, saying, "Lord, *'be merciful to me a sinner'* (Luke 18:13)."

The only reason a man thinks he is righteous is that he does not know the Law. You think you have never broken it because you do not understand it. There are some of you most respectable people who think you have been so good that you can go to heaven by your own works. You would not exactly say so, but you secretly think so; you have devoutly taken the sacrament, you have been mightily pious in attending your church or chapel regularly, you are good to the poor, generous and upright, and you say, "I will be saved by my works." No, friend, look to the flame that Moses saw, and shrink, tremble, and despair. The Law can do nothing for us except condemn us. The utmost it can do is to whip us out of our boasted self-righteousness and drive us to

---

7. See Psalm 19:7 KJV, NKJV.

Christ. It puts a burden on our backs and makes us ask Christ to take it off. It is like a lancet; it probes the wound. It is, to use a parable, like a dark cellar that has not been opened for years and is full of all kinds of loathsome creatures. We may walk through it not knowing they are there. But the Law comes, opens the shutters, and lets light in; then we discover what vile hearts we have and how unholy our lives have been. Then, instead of boasting, we are made to fall on our faces and cry, "Lord, save me or I perish. Oh, save me for Your mercy's sake, or else I will be cast away."

Oh, you self-righteous ones now present, who think yourselves so good that you can go to heaven by your works—blind horses, perpetually going round the mill and making not one inch of progress—do you think to take the Law upon your shoulders as Sampson did the gates of Gaza? Do you imagine that you can perfectly keep this Law of God? Will you dare to say that you have not broken it? No, surely, you will confess, although in an undertone, "I have revolted." Then, know this: The Law can do nothing for you in the matter of forgiveness. All it can do is make you feel you are nothing at all. It can strip you; it can bruise you; it can kill you—but it can neither quicken, nor clothe, nor cleanse. It was never meant to do that.

Are you sad this morning, my hearer, because of sin? Do you feel that you have been guilty? Do you acknowledge your transgression? Do you confess your wandering? Hear me, then, as God's ambassador: God has mercy upon sinners. Jesus Christ came into the world to save sinners. And though you have broken the Law, He has kept it. Take His righteousness to be yours. Cast yourself upon Him. Come to Him now, stripped and naked, and take His robe as your covering. Come to Him, black and filthy, and wash yourself in the fountain opened for sin and uncleanness; and then you will know "What purpose does the Law serve?" That is the first point.

TO SLAY ALL HOPE OF SALVATION BY WORKS

Second, *the Law serves to slay all hope of salvation from a reformed life*. Most men, when they discover themselves to be guilty, vow that they will reform. They say, "I have been guilty and have deserved God's wrath, but for the future I will seek to perform enough good works to counterbalance all my old sins." In steps the Law, puts its hand on the sinner's mouth, and says, "Stop, you cannot do that. It is impossible."

I will show you how the Law does this. It does it partly by reminding the man that *future obedience can be no atonement for past guilt*. To use a common metaphor so that you may thoroughly understand me, imagine that you have run up a debt at your shop. Well, you cannot pay it. You go to Mrs. Brown, your shopkeeper, and you say to her, "Well, I am sorry, ma'am, that since my husband is out of work," and all that, "I know I will never be able to pay you. I owe you a very great debt, but, if you please, ma'am, if you will forgive me this debt I will never get into your debt anymore; I will always pay for all I have." "Yes," she would say, "but that will not square our accounts. If you do pay for all you have, it would be no more than you ought to do. But what about the old bills? How are they to be paid? They won't be paid by all your fresh payments." That is just what men do toward God. "True," they say, "I have gone far astray, I know; but I won't do so anymore." Ah, it was time you threw away such child's talk. You only manifest your rampant folly by such a hope. Can you wipe away your transgression by future obedience? Ah, no. The old debt must be paid somehow. God's justice is inflexible, and the Law tells you all your requirements can make no atonement for the past. You must have an atonement through Christ Jesus the Lord.

"But," says the man, "I will try and be better, and then I think I will have mercy given to me." Then the Law steps in and says, "You are going to try and keep me, are you? Why, man, you cannot do it." *Perfect obedience in the future is impossible*. The Ten Commandments are held up, and if any awakened sinner will but look at them, he will turn away and say, "It is impossible for me to keep them." "Why, man, you say you will be obedient in the future. You have not been obedient in the past, and there is no likelihood that you will keep God's Commandments in time to come. You say you will avoid the evils of the past. You cannot. 'Can the Ethiopian change his skin, or the leopard his spots? then may ye also do good, that are accustomed to do evil' (Jeremiah 13:23)." But you say, "I will take greater heed to my ways." "Sir, you will not; the temptation that overcame you yesterday will overcome you tomorrow. But, mark this, even if you could, you could not win salvation by it." The Law tells you that unless you perfectly obey you cannot be saved by your doings. It tells you that one sin will make a flaw in it all, that one transgression will spoil your whole obedience. You must wear a spotless garment in heaven. God can accept only an unbroken Law. So then, the Law answers this purpose: to tell men that their acquirements, their amendments, and their doings are of no use whatever in the matter of salvation. It is theirs to come to Christ, to get a new heart and a right spirit, to get the evangelical repentance that need not be repented of, so that they may put their trust in Jesus and receive pardon through His blood.

"What purpose does the Law serve?" It serves this purpose, as Luther said, the purpose of a hammer. Luther, you know, was very strong on the subject of the Law. He said,

> For if anyone is not a murderer, an adulterer, or a thief, and outwardly refrains from sin, as the Pharisee that is mentioned in the Gospel did, he would swear that he is righteous, and, therefore, he conceives an opinion of righteousness, and presumes of his good works and merits. Such a one God cannot otherwise mollify and humble, that he may acknowledge his misery and damnation, except by the Law, for that is the hammer of death, the thundering of hell, and the lightning of God's wrath, which beats to powder the obstinate and senseless hypocrites. For as long as the opinion of righteousness abides in man, so long there abides also in him incomprehensible pride, presumption, security, hatred of God, contempt of His grace and mercy, ignorance

of the promises and of Christ. The preaching of free remission of sins, through Christ, cannot enter into the heart of such a one, neither can he feel any taste or savor thereof; for that mighty rock and adamant wall, that is, the opinion of righteousness, wherewith the heart is environed, resists it. Therefore, the Law is that hammer, that fire, that mighty strong wind, and that terrible earthquake rending the mountains and breaking the rocks (1 Kings 19:11–13), that is to say, the proud and obstinate hypocrites. Elijah, not being able to abide these terrors of the Law, which by these things are signified, covered his face with his mantle. Notwithstanding, when the tempest ceased, of which he was a beholder, there came a soft and a gracious wind, in the which the Lord was; but it was necessary that the tempest of fire and of wind, and the earthquake, should pass, before the Lord revealed Himself in that gracious wind.

TO SHOW MAN THE MISERY OF SIN

The grace of God must follow me in this next step. *The Law is intended to show man the misery that will fall upon him through his sin.* I speak from experience, though I am young, and many of you who hear me will hear this with ears of attention because you have felt the same. There was a time with me, when I was younger, that I felt with much sorrow the evil of sin. My bones waxed old with my roaring all day long. Day and night, God's hand was heavy upon me. There was a time when He seared me with visions and affrighted me by dreams. By day I hungered for deliverance, for my soul fasted within me. I feared lest the very skies should fall upon me and crush my guilty soul. God's Law had gotten a hold upon me and was heaping me with misery. If I slept at night, I dreamed of the bottomless pit, and when I awoke, I seemed to feel the misery I had dreamed. Up to God's house I went; my song was but a groan. To my chamber I retired, and there with tears and groans I offered up my prayer, without a hope and without a refuge. I

THE USES OF THE LAW 49

could then say with David, "The owl is my partner and the bittern is my companion" (see Isaiah 34:11), for God's Law was flogging me with its ten-thonged whip and then rubbing me with brine afterward, so that I shook and quivered with pain and anguish, and my soul chose strangling rather than life, for I was exceedingly sorrowful.

Some of you have had the same. The Law was sent on purpose to do that. But, you will ask, "Why that misery?" I answer that misery was sent for this reason: to make me cry to Jesus. Our heavenly Father does not usually make us seek Jesus until He has whipped us clean out of all our confidence; He cannot make us seek earnestly after heaven until He has made us feel something of the intolerable tortures of an aching conscience, which has foretaste of hell. Do you not remember, my hearer, when you used to awake in the morning, and the first thing you took up was *Alleine's Alarm,* or *Baxter's Call to the Unconverted?* Oh, those books, those books! In my childhood I read and devoured them when under a sense of guilt, but they were like sitting at the foot of Sinai. When I turned to Baxter, I found him saying some such things as these:

Sinner, think—within an hour you may be in hell. Think—you may soon be dying. Death is even now gnawing at your cheek. What will you do when you stand before the bar of God without a Savior? Will you tell Him you had no time to spend on religion? Will that empty excuse not melt into thin air? Oh, sinner, will you then dare to insult your Maker? Will you then dare to scoff at Him? Think—the flames of hell are hot and the wrath of God is heavy. Were your bones made of steel and your ribs of brass, you might quiver with fear. Oh, if you had the strength of a giant, you could not wrestle with the Most High. What will you do when He tears you in pieces, and there is no one to deliver you? What will you do when He fires off His ten great guns at you?[8] The first commandment will say, "Crush him; he has broken me!" The second will say, "Damn him; he has broken me!" The third will say, "A curse upon him; he has broken me!" And so they will all fly upon you; and you without a shelter, without a place to flee to, and without a hope.

You have not forgotten the days when no hymn seemed suitable to you but the one that began,

> "Stoop down my soul that used to rise,
> Converse awhile with death.
> Think how a gasping mortal lies,
> And pants away his breath."

Or else,

> "That awful day shall surely come,
> The 'pointed hour makes haste,
> When I must stand before my Judge,
> And pass the solemn test."

That was why the Law was sent—to convince us of sin, to make us shake and shiver before God. You who are self-righteous, let me speak to you this morning with just a word or two of terrible and burning earnestness. Remember, sirs, the day is coming when a crowd more vast than this will be assembled on the plains of earth; when the Savior, Judge

---

8. "There is a war between you and God's Law. The Ten Commandments are against you. The first comes forward and says, 'Let him be cursed. For he denies Me. He has another god beside Me. His god is his belly, and he yields his homage to his lust.' All the Ten Commandments, like ten great cannons, are pointed at you today. For you have broken all of God's statutes and lived in daily neglect of all His commands. Soul, you will find it a hard thing to go at war with the Law. When the Law came in peace, Sinai was covered in smoke, and even Moses said, '*I exceedingly fear and quake!*' (Hebrews 12:21). What will you do when the Law of God comes in terror, when the trumpet of the archangel tears you from your grave, when the eyes of God burn their way into your guilty soul, when the great books are opened and all your sin and shame are punished....Can you stand against an angry Law in that Day?" *Charles Spurgeon*

of men, will sit on a Great White Throne. Now, He is come. The book is opened. The glory of heaven is displayed, rich with triumphant love and burning with unquenchable vengeance. Ten thousand angels are on either hand, and you are standing to be tried. Now, self-righteous man, tell me now that you went to church three times a day! Come, man, tell me now that you kept all the Commandments! Tell me now that you are not guilty! Come before Him with a proof of your works, your anise, and your cummin! (See Matthew 23:23.) Come along with you! What is your response? Where are you going? Oh, you are fleeing. You are crying, "Rocks, hide us; mountains on us fall." (See Revelation 6:16.) What are you doing, man? Why, you were so fair on earth that none dared to speak to you. You were so good and so comely; why do you run away? Come, man, pluck up courage. Come before your Maker, and tell Him that you were honest, sober, and excellent and that you deserve to be saved! Why do you delay to repeat your boastings? Out with it— come, say it! No, you will not. I see you still flying, with shrieks, away from your Maker's presence. There will be none found to stand before Him, then, in their own righteousness.

But look! I see a man coming forward out of that motley throng. He marches forward with a steady step and a smiling eye. Is there any man found who will dare to approach the dread tribunal of God? Is there one who dares to stand before his Maker? Yes, there is one. He comes forward and cries, *"Who shall lay any thing to the charge of God's elect?"* (Romans 8:33). Do you not shudder? Will the mountains of wrath swallow him? Will not God launch that dreadful thunderbolt against him? No; listen while he confidently proceeds: *"Who is he that condemneth? It is Christ that died, yea rather, that is risen again"* (v. 34). And I see the right hand of God outstretched—"Come, you blessed, enter the kingdom prepared for you." Now, the verse that you once sweetly sang is fulfilled—

Bold shall I stand in that great day,
For who aught to my charge shall lay,

While, through Thy blood, absolv'd I am
From sin's tremendous curse and shame?

TO SHOW THE WORLD THE VALUE OF A SAVIOR

And now, my dear friends, I am afraid of wearying you; therefore, let me briefly hint at one other thought. "What purpose does the Law serve?" *It was sent into the world to show the value of a Savior.* Just as foils set off jewels and as dark spots make bright tints more bright, so the Law makes Christ appear fairer and more heavenly. I hear the Law of God curse man—how harsh its voice is. Jesus says, "Come to Me." Oh, what music! It is all the more musical after the discord of the Law. I see the Law condemns; I behold Christ obeying it. Oh, how ponderous that price—when I know how weighty was the demand! I read the commandments, and I find them strict and awfully severe—how holy must Christ have been to obey all these for me! Nothing makes me value my Savior more than seeing the Law condemn me. When I know this Law stands in my way and, like a flaming cherubim, will not let me enter paradise, then I can tell how sweetly precious Jesus Christ's righteousness, which is a passport to heaven and gives me grace to enter there, must be.

TO KEEP MEN FROM SELF-RIGHTEOUSNESS

And, last, "What purpose, then, does the Law serve?" It was sent into the world *to keep Christian men from self-righteousness.* Christian men—do they ever get self-righteous? Yes, they do. The best Christian man in the world will find it hard work to keep himself from boasting and being self-righteous. On his deathbed, John Knox was attacked with self-righteousness. The last night of his life on earth, he slept for a few hours, during which he uttered many deep and heavy moans. Being asked why he moaned so deeply, he replied, "I have during my life sustained many assaults of Satan, but at present he has assaulted me most fearfully and put forth all his strength to make an end of me at once.

The cunning serpent has labored to persuade me that I have merited heaven and eternal blessedness by the faithful discharge of my ministry. But blessed be God, who has enabled me to quench this fiery dart by suggesting to me such passages as these: '*What hast thou that thou didst not receive?*' (1 Corinthians 4:7) and, '*By the grace of God I am what I am*' (1 Corinthians 15:10)." Yes, and each of us have felt the same.

I have often felt myself rather amused at some of my brothers and sisters who have come to me and said, "I trust the Lord will keep you humble," when they themselves were not only as proud as they were high, but a few inches over. They have been most sincere in prayer that I should be humble, unwittingly nursing their own pride by their own imaginary reputation for humility. I have long since given up entreating people to be humble because it naturally tends to make them proud. A man is apt to say, "Dear me, these people are afraid I will be proud; I must have something to be proud of." Then we say to ourselves, "I will not let them see it," and we try to keep our pride down; but we are, after all, as proud as Lucifer within. I find that the proudest and most self-righteous people are those who do nothing at all and have no shadow of presence for any opinion of their own goodness.

The old truth in the book of Job is true now. You know that in the beginning of the book of Job it is said, "*The oxen were plowing, and the asses feeding beside them*" (Job 1:14). That is generally the way in this world. The oxen are plowing in the church—we have some who are laboring hard for Christ—and the asses are feeding beside them, on the finest livings and the fattest of the land. These are the people who have so much to say about self-righteousness. What do they do? They do not do enough to earn a living, and yet they think they are going to earn heaven. They sit down and fold their hands, and yet they are so reverently righteous because they sometimes dole out a little in charity. They do nothing, and yet boast of self-righteousness. And with Christian people it is the same. If God makes you laborious and keeps you constantly engaged in His service, you are less likely to be proud of your self-righteousness than you are if you do nothing. But at all times there is a natural tendency to it. Therefore, God has written the Law, that when we read it we may see our faults; that when we look into it, as into a looking glass, we may see the impurities in our flesh and have reason to abhor ourselves in sackcloth and ashes and cry to Jesus for mercy. Use the Law in this fashion, and in no other.

And now, says one, "Sir, are there any here that you have been preaching at?" Yes, I like to preach at people. I do not believe it is of any avail to preach *to* people; preach right into them and right at them. In every circle I find a class who say, in plain English, "Well, I am as good a father as is to be found in the parish. I am a good tradesman. I tithe and give offerings. I am no rogue or atheist. I go to church, or I go to chapel, and that is more than everybody does. I donate money to charity. I say my prayers. Therefore, I believe I stand as good a chance of heaven as anybody in the world." I do believe that three out of four of the people of London think something of that sort. Now, if that is the ground of your trust, you have a rotten hope; you have a plank to stand upon that will not bear your weight in the Day of God's account. As the Lord my God lives, before whom I stand, *"except your righteousness shall exceed the righteousness of the scribes and Pharisees, ye shall in no case enter into the kingdom of heaven"* (Matthew 5:20). And if you think the best performance of your hands can save you, know that *"Israel, which followed after the law of righteousness, hath not attained to the law of righteousness"* (Romans 9:31). Those who did not seek after it have attained it. Why? Because the one has sought it by faith, the other has sought it by the deeds of the Law, where justification was never to be found. Hear now the Gospel, men and women; down with that boasting form of your righteousness; away with your hopes, with all your trusts that spring from this—

> Could your tears forever flow,
> Could your zeal no respite know,
> All for sin could not atone;
> Christ must save, and save alone.

If you would know how we must be saved, hear this—you must come to Christ with nothing of your own. Christ has kept the Law. You are to have His righteousness as your righteousness. Christ has suffered in the place of all who repent. His punishment is to stand instead of your being punished. And through faith in the sanctification and atonement of Christ, you are to be saved. Come, then, you weary and heavy laden, bruised and mangled by the Fall. Come then, you sinners. Come, then, you moralists. Come, then, all you who have broken God's Law and feel it. Leave your own trusts and come to Jesus. He will take you in, give you a spotless robe of righteousness, and make you His forever. "But how can I come?" says one. "Must I go home and pray?" No, friend. Where you are standing now, you may come to the Cross. Oh, if you know yourself to be a sinner, I beseech you, before your foot leaves the floor on which you stand—now—say this,

Myself into Your arms I cast:
Lord, save my guilty soul at last.

Now, down with you, away with your self-righteousness. Look to me—look, now. Do not say, "Must I mount to heaven and bring Christ down?" (See Romans 10:6.) "The word is near you, on your mouth and in your heart; if you confess with your mouth the Lord Jesus, and believe with your heart, you will be saved." (See verses 8–9.) Yes, you—you—you. I bless God, we have heard of hundreds who have in this place believed in Christ. Some of the darkest souls of the human race have come to me just recently and told me what God has done for them. Oh, that you, too, would now come to Jesus. Remember, he who believes will be saved, though his sins be many; and he who does not believe must perish, though his sins be few. Oh, that the Holy Spirit would lead you to believe, and you will escape the wrath to come and have a place in paradise among the redeemed!

George Whitefield was "the man"! When it comes to breaking out of stuffy tradition and proclaiming the Truth with boldness and courage, this young man led the pack. His fresh, unconventional ideas produced both conversion in and contempt from his hearers. Just like every great man of God, George Whitefield was a radical—free from the chains of religious tradition, serving the Master with a passion.

—Kirk

GEORGE WHITEFIELD

One of the most outstanding preachers of his time, George Whitefield labored in the Gospel for thirty-five years and opened the way for what has been termed "mass evangelism."

George Whitefield was born on December 16, 1714, in Gloucester, England, the son of a wine merchant and innkeeper. When he was a young man, Whitefield developed a deep hunger for God. Though he was a poor student, he had a great desire to preach. As a result, he fasted regularly, prayed often, attended public worship sometimes twice a day, and read books, which led him "directly into an experimental knowledge of Jesus Christ." In 1735, at twenty-one years of age, he was converted after reading *The Life of God in the Soul of Man*, which Charles Wesley had loaned him. He wrote, "God was pleased…to remove the heavy load and enable me to lay hold of His Son by a living faith." Shortly afterward, he entered Oxford University, where he fellowshipped with the Wesley brothers, John and Charles. His ministry began with his preaching in jails to the prisoners and doing missionary work in the colony of Georgia. In 1743, he parted company with the Wesleys over doctrinal disagreements and adopted a moderate Calvinism.

His first sermon brought several different reactions. Some were impressed by his fervor, while others mocked. Some complained to the bishop that his sermon had driven fifteen people "mad," which we would understand today to mean that they had been converted. The bishop replied by saying that he hoped the "madness" would not be forgotten before the next Sunday!

Word soon got around that Whitefield was an exciting and effective preacher, and invitations began to come in. Several churches, however, actually closed their pulpits to him. Undaunted, Whitefield continued to preach the same message: the new birth and justification by faith. To many it was a novel and even wicked message. Since it was straight from the Bible, Whitefield had no qualms about presenting it.

Whitefield was the most traveled preacher of the Gospel up to this time. He made thirteen trips across the Atlantic to visit the American colonies, and he traveled around England and Scotland, stopping here and there to deliver his sermons. He spent twenty-four years of ministry in the British Isles and nine more in America, speaking to some ten million souls. He also saw some of the great events of his day, including the "great revivals." When he visited Glasgow, he attended two communion services, one of which attracted twenty thousand people.

Whitefield delivered more than eighteen thousand sermons in his lifetime, an average of five hundred a year, or ten each week. One of his favorite preaching places was just outside London, on a great open tract of land known as Moorfiends. He had no designated time for his services, but whenever he began to preach, thousands came to hear. Not all were fans, and he would often say, "I was honored with having stones, dirt, rotten eggs, and pieces of dead cats thrown at me." Several times, he was also attacked physically, being beaten or having bricks thrown at him. Afterward, he said, "We are all immortal until our work is done," a phrase he would often repeat.

The thousands of converts during his ministry were the result of his extensive preaching in Scotland and Wales, and visits to America. Benjamin Franklin became a good friend of the evangelist, and he was always impressed with the preaching, although he never converted. Once Franklin emptied his pockets at home, knowing that an offering would be taken. But it was to no avail. So powerful was the appeal at Whitefield's meeting that Franklin ended up borrowing money from a stranger sitting nearby to put in the plate!

Whitefield's voice could be heard at a range of one mile without amplification, and it is said that his oratorical powers were such that he could make an audience weep with his pronunciation. On a balcony not far from his deathbed, he preached his last message to more than two thousand people and died within an hour after extending the invitation.

Toward the end of his life he made every effort to be at peace with other Christians, especially the Wesleys and said, "Let the name of Whitefield perish and that of Christ be glorified, and let me be but the servant of all!" Perhaps the one sad aspect to his life was his workload. He had a tough schedule of travel and preaching tours, and it was this load of commitments that finally wore him out. He died on September 30, 1770, in Newburyport, Massachusetts.

His funeral sermon was preached by John Wesley, who spoke of Whitefield's tenderheartedness and charitableness and "the love of God shed abroad in his heart, filling his soul with tender, disinterested love to every child of man."

THE LORD OUR RIGHTEOUSNESS

George Whitefield

"THE LORD OUR RIGHTEOUSNESS."
—Jeremiah 23:6

Whoever is acquainted with the nature of mankind in general, or the predisposition of his own heart in particular, must acknowledge that self-righteousness is the last idol that is rooted out of the heart. Being born under a covenant of works, it is natural for us all to turn to a covenant of works for our everlasting salvation. And we have inherited such devilish pride by our fall from God that we would glory—if not wholly, at least in part—in being the cause of our own salvation. We cry out against the idea that we can, in some way, merit salvation, and that very justly, but we are all believers in it by nature. It is, therefore, no wonder so many natural men embrace that idea. It is true that we disclaim the doctrine of merit and are ashamed to say directly that we deserve any good at the hands of God. Therefore, as the apostle excellently observed, "We go about to establish a righteousness of our own, and," like the Pharisees of old, "we will not wholly submit to the righteousness that is from God through Jesus Christ our Lord." (See Romans 10:3.)

This is the most distressing and also—alas!—the most common evil that was ever yet seen under the sun. An evil that in any age, especially in these dregs of time in which we live, cannot sufficiently be railed against. For as it is with the people, so it is with the priests; and it is to be feared, even in those places the truth as it is in Jesus was once eminently preached, that many ministers are so sadly degenerated from their pious ancestors that the doctrines of grace, especially the personal, *all-sufficient righteousness* of Jesus, are too seldom and too slightly mentioned. Therefore, the love of many grows cold. I have often thought that if it were for this single consideration to raise our venerable forefathers again from their graves, they would thunder the fatal error of today's preachers in their ears.

The righteousness of Jesus Christ is one of those great mysteries that even the angels desire to investigate further. It seems to be one of the first lessons that God taught men after the Fall. For, what were the coats that God made to put on our first parents, but models of the application of the merits of the righteousness of Jesus Christ to believers' hearts? We are told that those coats were made of skins of beasts (Genesis 3:21), and as beasts were not then food for men, we may fairly infer that those beasts were slain in sacrifice, in commemoration of the great Sacrifice, Jesus Christ, that would one day be offered. And as Adam and Eve put on the skins of the beasts thus slain, they were taught how their nakedness was to be covered with the righteousness of the Lamb of God.

This is what is meant when we are told, *"Abraham believed God, and it was accounted to him for righteousness"* (Galatians 3:6). In short, this is it of which both the Law and the prophets have spoken of, especially Jeremiah in the words of the text *"THE LORD OUR RIGHTEOUSNESS."*

I propose, through divine grace,

1.   to consider who is meant by the word *"LORD."*

2.   to consider how the Lord is man's righteousness.

3. to consider some of the chief objections that are generally urged against this doctrine.

4. to show some very ill consequences that flow naturally from denying this doctrine.

5. to conclude with an exhortation to all to come to Christ by faith, that they may be enabled to say with the prophet in the text, "THE LORD OUR RIGHTEOUSNESS."

WHO IS MEANT BY THE WORD "LORD"

If any followers of Socinians[9] are drawn by curiosity to hear what this babbler has to say, let them be ashamed of denying the divinity of that Lord who has bought poor sinners with His precious blood. For the person mentioned in the text as *"the LORD"* is Jesus Christ.

> *Behold, the days come, saith the LORD, that I will raise unto David a righteous Branch, and a King shall reign and prosper, and shall execute judgment and justice in the earth. In his days Judah shall be saved, and Israel shall dwell safely: and this is his name whereby he shall be called, THE LORD OUR RIGHTEOUSNESS.*
>
> (Jeremiah 23:5–6)

By the righteous Branch, all agree that we are to understand Jesus Christ. It is He who is called *"the LORD"* in our text. If there were no other text in the Bible to prove the divinity of Christ, this one is sufficient, for if the word *Lord* may properly belong to Jesus Christ, He must be God. And, as it says in the margin of your Bibles, the word *Lord* in the original language is *Jehovah*, which is the essential title of God Himself. Come then, kiss the Son of God, bow down before Him, and honor Him, even as you honor the Father. Learn from the angels,

---

9. An adherent of a sixteenth and seventeenth century theological movement that professed belief in God and adherence to the Scriptures but denied the divinity of Christ and therefore also denied the Trinity.

those morning stars, and worship Him as truly God. Otherwise you are idolaters as those who worship statues. And as for you who say Christ was a mere man and yet profess that He was your Savior, according to your own principles, you are accursed. For, if Christ was a mere man, then He is only an arm of flesh. It is written, "Cursed is he who trusts in an arm of flesh." (See Jeremiah 17:5.) But I would hope that there are no such monsters here or, at least, that, after these considerations, they would be ashamed of expressing such monstrous absurdities anymore. For it is plain that the word "LORD" means the Lord Jesus Christ, who here claims for Himself the title Jehovah and, therefore, must be very God of very God or, as the apostle devoutly expressed it, "*God blessed for ever*" (Romans 9:5).

HOW THE LORD IS TO BE MAN'S RIGHTEOUSNESS

And that is, in one word, by *imputation*. For it pleased God, after He had made all things by the word of His power, to create man after His own image. And so infinite was the condescension of the high and lofty One who inhabits eternity that, although He might have insisted on everlasting obedience from man in all his future generations, He was pleased to constrain Himself by a covenant or agreement made with His own creatures to give them immortality and eternal life in return for their unsinning obedience. For when it is said, "*The day that thou eatest thereof thou shalt surely die*" (Genesis 2:17), we may fairly infer that as long as he continued to be obedient and did not eat of the Tree, he would surely live. The third chapter of Genesis gives us a full, but mournful, account of how our first parents broke this covenant and, as a result, stood in need of a better righteousness than their own in order to procure their future acceptance with God. For what must they do? They were as much under a covenant of works as ever. And though, after their disobedience, they were without strength, yet they were obliged not only to do, but also to continue to do, all things, in the most perfect manner, that the Lord had required of them. And not only did they have to do so, but they also had to satisfy God's infinitely offended justice for the breach they had already been guilty of. Here then opens the amazing scene of *divine philanthropy*; I mean, God's love to man. For behold, what man could not do, Jesus Christ, the Son of His Father's love, undertook to do for him. And that God might be just in justifying the ungodly, He, though *"being in the form of God, thought it not robbery to be equal with God: but…took upon him the form of a servant"* (Philippians 2:6–7), even human nature. In that nature He obeyed and, by this, fulfilled the whole moral Law in our stead. Moreover, He also died a painful death upon the cross, thereby becoming a curse for those whom the Father had given to Him. As God, He satisfied the Law at the same time that He obeyed and suffered as man. Being God and man in one person, He worked a full, perfect, and sufficient righteousness for all to whom it was to be given.

Here then we see the meaning of the word *"RIGHTEOUSNESS."* It implies the active, as well as passive, obedience of the Lord Jesus Christ. Generally speaking, when talking of the merits of Christ, we mention only the latter (His death) when the former (His life and active obedience) is equally necessary. Christ is not a sufficient Savior for us unless we join both together. Christ not only died, but lived— not only suffered, but obeyed—for poor sinners. And both these together make up a complete righteousness, which is to be imputed to us, just as the disobedience of our first parents was imputed to us. In this sense, and no other, we are to understand that parallel that the apostle Paul drew, in the fifth chapter of Romans, between the first and Second Adam. This is what he elsewhere termed our being *"made the righteousness of God in him"* (2 Corinthians 5:21). This is the sense in which the prophet would have us understand the words of the text. Therefore, *"she* [the church] *shall be called* [having this righteousness imputed to her], *The* LORD *our righteousness"* (Jeremiah 33:16). I think this is a passage worthy of the profoundest meditation of all the sons and daughters of Abraham.

The proud hearts of fallen men are continually urging many objections against this wholesome, divine, and soul-saving doctrine.

THE CHIEF OBJECTIONS AGAINST THIS DOCTRINE

First, men who wish to appear as friends of morality would say that the doctrine of an imputed righteousness is "destructive of good works and leads to licentiousness."

And who, I ask, are the persons who generally urge this objection? Are they men full of faith, and men really concerned for good works? No. Almost without exception, they are notoriously men of corrupt minds, reprobate in the faith. The best title I can give them is that of *profane moralists*, or moralists called falsely. I appeal to the experience of the present as well as past ages: Iniquity most abounds where the doctrine of Christ's whole personal righteousness is most rejected and left unmentioned. Anti-Christian principles always did and always will lead to anti-Christian practices. Never was there a reformation brought about in the church, except by preaching the doctrine of an imputed righteousness. The man of God, Luther, called it "the article by which the church stands or falls." And though the preachers of this doctrine are generally branded by those on the other side with the scurrilous names of Antinomians or deceivers and so on, I believe that if the truth of the doctrine on both sides was to be judged by the lives of those who profess to believe it, on our side the question would have the advantage every way.

It is true that this, as well as every other doctrine of grace, may be abused. And perhaps the unchristian walk of some who have talked of Christ's imputed righteousness, justification by faith, and the like, without ever feeling it imputed to their own souls, has given the enemies of the Lord thus cause to blaspheme. But this is a very unsafe as well as a very unfair way of arguing. The only question should be whether or not this doctrine of an imputed righteousness does in itself cut off the occasion of good works or lead to immoral behavior. To this we may boldly answer, In no way. It excludes works, indeed, from being any cause of our justification in the sight of God, but it requires good works as a proof of our having this righteousness imputed to us and as a declarative evidence of our justification in the sight of men. (See James 2:20–26.) How can the doctrine of an imputed righteousness be a doctrine leading to licentiousness?

It is all slander. The apostle Paul introduced an infidel making this objection in his epistle to the Romans, and none but infidels who never felt the power of Christ's resurrection upon their souls will urge it ever again. And, therefore, notwithstanding this objection, with the prophet in the text, we may boldly say, *"THE LORD OUR RIGHTEOUSNESS."*

Satan (and no wonder that his servants imitate him) often transforms himself into *"an angel of light"* (2 Corinthians 11:14). Therefore, in order to dress their objections in the best colors, some urge that "our Savior preached no such doctrine; that in His Sermon on the Mount, He mentions only morality." Consequently, the doctrine of an imputed righteousness falls wholly to the ground.

But surely the men who urge this objection either never have read— or never understood—our Lord's blessed discourse, in which the doctrine of an imputed righteousness is so plainly taught that he who lives, if he has eyes that see, may read.

Indeed, our Lord did recommend morality and good works (as all faithful ministers will do) and cleared the moral Law from many corrupt glosses put upon it by the letter-learned Pharisees. But then, before He came to this, remarkably, He spoke of inward piety—such as poverty of spirit, meekness, holy mourning, purity of heart, and especially hungering and thirsting after righteousness. Then He recommended good works as evidence of our having His righteousness imputed to us and these graces and divine tempers written in our hearts. *"Let your light* [that is, the divine light I have been mentioning] *so shine before men"* in a holy life *"that they may see your good works, and glorify your Father which is in heaven"* (Matthew 5:16). And then He immediately added, *"Think not that I am come to destroy the* [moral] *law…: I am not come to destroy* [to take away the force of it as a rule of life], *but to fulfill* [to obey it in its whole latitude, and give the complete sense of it]" (v. 17). And then He went on to show how exceedingly broad the moral Law is.[10] So our Lord, instead of setting aside an imputed righteousness in His Sermon on the Mount, not only confirmed it, but also answered the preceding objection urged against it by making good works a proof and evidence of its being imputed to our souls. Therefore, he who has ears to hear, let him hear what the prophet said in the words of the text, "THE LORD OUR RIGHTEOUSNESS."

Satan not only quoted Scripture, but also backed one temptation after another with it when he attacked Christ in the wilderness. His children generally take the same method in treating his doctrine. And, therefore, they urge another objection against the doctrine of an imputed righteousness from the example of the young man in the gospel.

---

10. "No one will deny that since God made man, He has a right to demand obedience from man. The fact that He has also given us both a natural and a written Law by which we are to be judged also cannot be questioned by anyone who believes Paul's epistle to the Romans was written in divine authority. In it we are told of a Law written in the heart and a Law given by Moses, and we are told that each of us has broken these Laws, which is evident from our sad and frequent experience. Accordingly, the Holy Scriptures inform us that *"there is no man which sinneth not"* (2 Chronicles 6:36), that *"in many things we offend all"* (James 3:2), and that *"if we say we have no sin, we deceive ourselves"* (1 John 1:8). And if we are thus offenders against God, it follows that we stand in need of forgiveness for thus offending Him—unless we think God enacts Laws and, at the same time, does not care whether they are obeyed or not. This is as absurd as a prince who would establish Laws for the proper government of his country and then reward every violator of them with immunity. But God has not dealt so foolishly with His creatures. No, just as He gave us a Law, He demands our obedience to that Law, and He has obliged us universally and perseveringly to obey it, under a penalty that is nothing less than His curse and eternal death for every breach of it. For thus speaks the scripture, *"Cursed is every one that continueth not in all things which are written in the book of the law to do them"* (Galatians 3:10). The Scripture also speaks in another place, *"The soul that sinneth, it shall die"* (Ezekiel 18:20). Now it has already been proven that we have all sinned. Therefore, unless some means can be found to satisfy God's justice, we must perish eternally." *George Whitefield*

We may state it thus: "Mark chapter 10 mentions a young man who came running to Christ to ask Him what he should do to inherit eternal life. Christ referred him to the Commandments, to know what he must do to inherit eternal life. It is plain, therefore, that works were to be, at least partly, the cause of his justification. Consequently, the doctrine of an imputed righteousness is unscriptural." This is the objection in its full strength—and little strength in all its fullness. For, if I were to prove the necessity of an imputed righteousness, I scarcely know how I could present a better example to prove its truth.

Let us take a closer view of this young man and of our Lord's behavior toward him. The Evangelist told us, "*When he [Christ] was gone forth into the way, there came one running*" (Mark 10:17). It seems he was a nobleman; a rarity indeed to see such a one running to Christ! Not only was he running, but he also "*kneeled to him*" (v. 17). Perhaps many of his rank now do know the time when they kneeled to Christ. The man asked and asked Jesus, "*Good Master, what shall I do that I may inherit eternal life?*" (Mark 10:17). Then Jesus, to see whether or not he believed Him to be who He really was—truly and properly God—said to him, "*Why callest thou me good? there is none good but one, that is, God*" (v. 18). And so that the man might directly answer His question, Christ said, "*Thou knowest the commandments, Do not commit adultery,...Do not bear false witness,...Defraud not,*[11]*...Honour thy father and thy mother*" (v. 19). This was a direct answer to his question, namely, that eternal life was not to be attained by his doings. By referring him to the Commandments, our Lord did not (as the objectors insinuate) hint in the least that the man's morality would award him the favor and mercy of God. Instead, Christ intended His statement to make the Law the man's schoolmaster in order to bring him to Himself. The young man, seeing how he had broken every one of these Commandments, might by this be convinced

---

11. It is strange that "defraud not" is not one of the "commandments." Perhaps Jesus was making reference to the source of this man's riches. It is beneficial indeed for us, as Christ's followers, to point out, in love, what we perceive to be evident personal sins in those to whom we speak.

of the insufficiency of his righteousness. Consequently, he would see the absolute necessity of looking for a better righteousness, on which he might depend for eternal life.

This was what our Lord intended. Being self-righteous and willing to justify himself, the young man said, "*All these have I observed from my youth*" (v. 20). If he had known himself, however, he would have confessed, "All these have I broken from my youth." For, though he had not actually committed adultery, had he never lusted after a woman in his heart?[12] Though he had not really killed another, had he never been angry without a cause or spoken unadvisedly with his lips? If so, by breaking one of the least Commandments in the least degree, he became accountable to the curse of God. The Law says, "*Cursed is **every** one that continueth not in all things which are written in the book of the law*" (Galatians 3:10, emphasis added). And, therefore, as observed before, our Lord was so far from speaking against imputed righteousness that He treated the young man in that manner on purpose to convince him of its necessity.

But perhaps they will reply, "It is said, '*Jesus beholding him, loved him*' (Mark 10:21)." And what then? This He might do with a human love, and at the same time this young man may have no interest in His blood. Thus Christ is said to wonder, to weep, over Jerusalem, and say, "Oh, that thou had known Me." But similar passages refer only to His human nature. There is a great deal of difference between the love Christ had for this young man, and the love He had for Mary, Lazarus, and their sister Martha.

---

12. "...for the Law must be preached to self-righteous sinners. We must take care of healing before we see sinners wounded, lest we should say, "Peace, peace," where there is no peace. (See Jeremiah 6:14; 8:11.) Secure sinners must hear the thunderings of Mount Sinai before we bring them to Mount Zion. Those who never preach the Law, it is to be feared, are unskillful in delivering the glad tidings of the Gospel. Every minister should be a Boanerges, a son of thunder, as well as a Barnabus, a son of consolation. There was an earthquake and a whirlwind before the small still voice came to Elijah. We must first show people they are condemned and then show them how they must be saved. But wisdom will direct how and when to preach the Law, and when to apply the promises of the Gospel." *George Whitefield*

To illustrate this by comparison: A minister of the Lord Jesus Christ sees many people with amiable dispositions—such as a readiness to hear the Word, a decent behavior at public worship, and a life outwardly spotless in many regards—and cannot help but love them. But there is a great difference between the love that a minister feels for such people and the divine love—the union and sympathy of soul—that he feels for those he is satisfied are really born again in God. Apply this to our Lord's case, as a faint illustration of it. Consider what has been said about the young man's case in general, and then, if you were fond of this objection before, instead of triumphing, now, like him, you will go away sorrowful. Our Savior's reply to him convinces us more and more of the truth of the prophet's assertion in the text that "the Lord is our righteousness."

But there is a fourth grand objection left, which is taken from Matthew 25, in which some might argue that "our Lord is described as rewarding people with eternal life because they fed the hungry, clothed the naked, and such. Their works, therefore, were a cause of their justification. Consequently, the doctrine of imputed righteousness is not agreeable to Scripture."

This, I confess, is the most plausible objection that is brought against the doctrine insisted on from the text. In order to answer it in as clear and brief a manner as possible, we confess with the Article of the Church of England,

> That although good works do not justify us, yet they will follow justification as fruits of it. Though they spring from faith in Christ and a renewed soul, they will receive a reward of grace, though not of debt. Consequently, the more we abound in such good works, the greater our reward will be when Jesus Christ comes to judge us.

Consider these, and they will help us to answer the objection now before us. Jesus said,

> *Then shall the King say unto them on his right hand, Come, ye blessed of my Father, inherit the kingdom prepared for you from the foundation of the world: for I was an hungered, and ye gave me meat: I was thirsty, and ye gave me drink: I was a stranger, and ye took me in: naked, and ye clothed me: I was sick, and ye visited me: I was in prison, and ye came unto me.* (Matthew 25:34–36)

The implication is that Christ will, therefore, reward those on His right because they have done these things out of love to Him and, therefore, have evidenced themselves to be His true disciples. It is evident that the people did not depend on these good actions for their justification in the sight of God. "*When saw we thee an hungered,*" they say, "*and fed thee? or thirsty, and gave thee drink? When saw we thee a stranger, and took thee in? or naked, and clothed thee? or when saw we thee sick, or in prison, and came unto thee?*" (vv. 37–39). The language they used and questions they asked are quite improper for persons who are relying on their own righteousness for acceptance and innocence in the sight of God.

But then they reply against you, "In the latter part of the chapter, it is plain that Jesus Christ rejects and damns the others for not doing these things. And, therefore, if He damns these for not doing, He saves those for doing. Consequently, the doctrine of an imputed righteousness is good for nothing."

But that is not logical at all. God may justly damn any man for omitting the least duty of the moral Law. In Himself, He is not obliged to give to anyone any reward, even if the man has done all that he can. Even the most holy souls living are unprofitable servants; we must admit that we have not done nearly as much as it was our duty to do. Therefore, from or in ourselves, we cannot be justified in the sight of God. This was the understanding of the devout souls just now referred to. Sensible of this, they were so far from depending on their works for justification in the sight of God that they were filled, as it were, with a holy blushing to think our Lord would condescend to mention, much more to reward them for, their poor works of faith and labors of love. I am persuaded their hearts would rise with a holy indignation against those who urge this passage as an objection to the assertion of the prophet, that "the Lord is our righteousness."

Thus, I think, we have fairly answered the grand objections that are generally argued against the doctrine of an imputed righteousness. If I were to stop here, I think I may say, *"We are more than conquerors through him that loved us"* (Romans 8:37). But there is a way of arguing that I have always admired. I have thought it always very convincing to show the *absurdities* that will follow from denying any particular proposition in dispute.

THE CONSEQUENCES OF DENYING THIS DOCTRINE

Never did greater or more absurdities flow from denying any doctrine than will flow from denying the doctrine of Christ's imputed righteousness.

First, if we deny this doctrine, we turn the truth—the Word of God—into a lie and utterly subvert all those Scriptures that say we are saved by grace; that it is not of works, lest any man should boast; that salvation is God's free gift, and that he who glories must glory only in the Lord. For if the personal righteousness of Jesus Christ is not the sole cause of my acceptance with God, if any work done by or foreseen in me was in the least to be joined with it or looked upon by God as a cause of acquitting my soul from guilt, then I have something of which I may glory in myself. Not boasting is excluded from the great work of our redemption, but that cannot be if we are enemies of the doctrine of an imputed righteousness. It would be endless to enumerate how many texts of Scripture must be false if this doctrine was not true. Let it suffice to affirm generally that if we deny an imputed righteousness, we may as well deny a divine revelation completely, for it is the alpha and omega, the beginning and the end, of the Book of God. We must either disbelieve that or believe what the prophet spoke in the text, that "the Lord is our righteousness."

But further: I observed at the beginning of this discourse that we are all Arminians by nature. And here I venture further to affirming that, if we deny the doctrine of an imputed righteousness, whatever we may style ourselves, we are really idolators in our hearts and deserve no other title from men.

Friends, what do you think of this? Suppose I came and told you that you must intercede with saints for them to intercede with God for you; would you not say that I deserved to be thrust out of the synagogue? I suppose you would. And why? Because, you would say, the intercession of Jesus Christ was sufficient in itself, without the intercession of saints, and that it was blasphemous to join their prayers with His, as though He was not sufficient.

Suppose I went a little further and told you that the death of Christ was not sufficient without your death being added to it—that you must die as well as Christ, join your death with His, and then it would be sufficient. Might you not then, with a holy indignation, throw dust in the air and justly call me a "setter forth of strange doctrines"? (See Acts 17:18.) And now then, if it is not only absurd, but also blasphemous to join the intercession of saints with the intercession of Christ, as though His intercession was not sufficient; or our death with the death of Christ, as though His death was not sufficient, judge if it is not equally absurd, equally blasphemous, to join our obedience, either wholly or in part, with the obedience of Christ, as if that was not sufficient. And if so, what absurdities will follow our denying that the Lord, both as to His active and passive obedience, is our righteousness?

I will mention one more absurdity that comes from denying this doctrine.

I remember a story of a certain prelate, who, after many vain arguments to convince the Earl of Rochester of the invisible realities of another world, took leave of his lordship with words such as these: "Well, my lord, if there is no hell, I am safe; but if there is to be such a thing as hell, what will become of you?" I apply this to those who oppose the doctrine now insisted on. If there is no such thing as the doctrine of an imputed righteousness, those who hold it and bring forth fruit unto holiness are safe. But if there is such a thing (as there certainly is), what will become of you who deny it? It is no difficult matter to determine. Your portion must be in the lake of fire and brimstone forever and ever. Since you will rely upon your works, by your works you will be judged. They will be weighed in the balance of the sanctuary, and they will be found wanting. By your works, therefore, you will be condemned, and, being out of Christ, you will find God to be a consuming fire to your poor wretched souls.

The great Stoddard, of Northampton in New England, has, therefore, well entitled a book that he wrote (and which I would take this opportunity to recommend), "The Safety of Appearing in the Righteousness of Christ." For why should I lean upon a broken reed, when I can have the Rock of ages that can never be moved to stand upon?

And now, before I come to a more particular application, give me leave, in the apostle's language, to cry out triumphantly, "Where is the scribe? where is the disputer?" (1 Corinthians 1:20). Where is the reasoning infidel of this generation? Can anything appear more reasonable, even according to your own way of arguing, than the doctrine here laid down? Have you not felt a convincing power go along with the Word? Why, then, will you not believe in the Lord Jesus Christ, so that He may become the Lord your righteousness?

But it is time for me to come a little closer to your consciences.

AN EXHORTATION TO FAITH

Friends, though some may be offended at this doctrine and may see it as foolish, many of you, I do not doubt, find it is precious, as it agrees with the style of sound words that you have learned to be true from your infancy. And, as the argument comes from a quarter you would have least expected, it may be received with more pleasure and satisfaction. But give me leave to ask you one question: Can you say, "THE LORD OUR RIGHTEOUSNESS"? I say, "THE LORD **OUR** RIGHTEOUSNESS." For, entertaining this doctrine in your heads without receiving the Lord Jesus Christ into your hearts to save you by a living faith will only increase your damnation. As I have often told you, so I tell you again, an unapplied Christ is no Christ at all. Can you then, with believing Thomas, cry out, "*My Lord and my God*" (John 20:28)?

Is Christ your sanctification as well as your outward righteousness? For the word "RIGHTEOUSNESS" in the text not only implies Christ's personal righteousness imputed to us, but also His holiness working in us. These two God has joined together. He never did, He never does, and He never will put them asunder. If you are justified by the blood, you are also sanctified by the Spirit of our Lord. Can you then in this sense say, "THE LORD OUR RIGHTEOUSNESS"? Were you ever made to abhor yourselves for your actual and original sins and to loathe your own righteousness? As the prophet beautifully expressed it, your righteousness is "*as filthy rags*" (Isaiah 64:6). Were you ever made to see and admire the all-sufficiency of Christ's righteousness and be excited by the Spirit of God to hunger and thirst after it? Could you ever say, "My soul is thirsty for Christ, yes, even for the righteousness of Christ? Oh, when will I come to appear before the presence of my God in the righteousness of Christ! Nothing but Christ! Nothing but Christ! Give me Christ, O God, and I am satisfied! My soul will praise You forever."

Was this ever the language of your hearts? And, after these inward conflicts, were you ever enabled to reach out the arm of faith and embrace the blessed Jesus in your souls, so that you could say, "*My beloved is mine,*

THE LORD OUR RIGHTEOUSNESS 77

and I am his?" (Song of Solomon 2:16). If so, fear not, whoever you are. Hail, all hail, you happy souls! The Lord, the Lord Christ, the everlasting God, is your righteousness. Christ has justified you; who condemns you? Christ has died for you—no, rather is risen again and ever lives to make intercession for you. Being now justified by His grace, you have peace with God, and will, before long, be with Jesus in glory, reaping everlasting and unspeakable fruits both in body and soul. For there is no condemnation to those who are really in Christ Jesus. "*Whether Paul or Apollos,…or life, or death,…all are yours; and ye are Christ's, and Christ is God's*" (1 Corinthians 3:22–23).

My friends, my heart is enlarged toward you! Oh, think of the love of Christ in dying for you! If the Lord is your righteousness, let the righteousness of your Lord be continually in your mouth. Talk of and recommend the righteousness of Christ when you lie down and when you rise up, at your going out and coming in! Think of the greatness of the gift, as well as the Giver! Show to all the world in whom you have believed! By your fruits, let all know that the Lord is your righteousness and that you are waiting for your Lord to return from heaven! Study to be holy, even as He who has called you and washed you in His own blood is holy! Do not let the righteousness of the Lord be spoken of as evil by you. Do not let Jesus be wounded in the house of His friends, but grow in grace and in the knowledge of our Lord and Savior Jesus Christ, day by day. Oh, think of His dying love! Let that love constrain you to obedience! Having been much forgiven, love much. Be always asking, "What can I do to express my gratitude to the Lord for giving me His righteousness?" Let that self-abasing, God-exalting question be always in your mouths: "Why me, Lord? Why me? Why am I taken and others left? Why is the Lord my righteousness? Why has He become my salvation, who have so often deserved damnation at His hands?"

My friends, I trust I feel somewhat of a sense of God's distinguishing love upon my heart; therefore, I must divert a little from congratulating you to invite poor Christless sinners to come to Him and accept His righteousness, so that they may have life.

Alas, my heart almost bleeds! What a multitude of precious souls are now before me! How shortly must all be ushered into eternity! And yet—O cutting thought! If God were now to require all your souls, how few, comparatively speaking, could really say, "THE LORD OUR RIGHTEOUSNESS"!

And do you think, O sinner, that you will be able to stand in the Day of Judgment, if Christ is not your righteousness? No, that alone is the wedding garment in which you must appear. (See Matthew 22:8–14.) O Christless sinners, I am distressed for you! The desires of my soul are enlarged.[13] Oh, that this may be an accepted time! That the Lord may be your righteousness! For where would you flee, if death were to find you naked? Indeed, there is no hiding yourselves from His presence. The pitiful fig leaves of your own righteousness will not cover your nakedness when God calls you to stand before Him. Adam found them ineffectual, and so will you. Oh, think of death! Oh, think of judgment![14] In just a little while, time will be no more. Then what will become of you, if the Lord is not your righteousness? Do you think that Christ will spare you? No, He who formed you will have no mercy on you. If you are not of Christ, if Christ is not your righteousness, Christ Himself will pronounce you damned. And can you bear to think of being damned by Christ? Can you bear to hear the Lord Jesus say to you, *"Depart from me, ye cursed, into everlasting fire, prepared for the devil and his angels"* (Matthew 25:41)? Can you live, do you think, in everlasting burnings? Is your flesh brass, and your bones iron? What if they

---

13. This reveals the secret of Whitefield's preaching. His words came from a tender, loving heart.
14. "First, we hear Moses' voice. We hear the voice of the Law. There is no going to Mount Zion but by the way of Mount Sinai. That is the right straight road. I know some say they do not know when they were converted. Those are, I believe, very few. Generally—no, I may say almost always—God deals otherwise. Some are, indeed, called sooner by the Lord than others, but before they are made to see the glory of God, they must hear the voice of the Law. So, too, you must hear the voice of the Law before you will ever be savingly called to God." *George Whitefield*

are? Hellfire, that fire prepared for the devil and his angels, will heat them through and through. And can you bear to depart from Christ? Oh, that heart-piercing thought![15] Ask those holy souls—who are at any time bewailing an absent God, who walk in darkness and see no light, though for only a few days or hours—ask them what it is like to lose the light and presence of Christ. See how they seek Him sorrowing, and go mourning after Him all the day long! And if it is so dreadful to lose the sensible presence of Christ only for a day, what must it be to be banished from Him for all eternity!

But thus it must be if Christ is not your righteousness. For God's justice must be satisfied, and unless Christ's righteousness is imputed and applied to you here, you must satisfy the divine justice in hell torments eternally. No, Christ Himself will condemn you to that place of torment. And how cutting is that thought! I think I see poor, trembling, Christless wretches standing before the judgment seat of God, crying out, "Lord, if we must be damned, let some angel, or some archangel, pronounce the damnatory sentence"—but all in vain. Christ Himself will pronounce the irrevocable sentence. Knowing, therefore, the terrors of the Lord, let me persuade you to close with Christ and never rest until you can say, "THE LORD OUR RIGHTEOUSNESS." Who knows? The Lord may have mercy on you and may abundantly pardon you. Beg God to give you faith, and if the Lord gives it to you, you will by it receive Christ, with His righteousness, and His all.

You do not need to fear the greatness or number of your sins. For are you sinners? So am I. Are you the chief of sinners? So am I. Are you backsliding sinners? So am I. And yet the Lord—forever adored be His rich, free, and sovereign grace—the Lord is my righteousness. Come then, O young man who is playing the Prodigal (as I acted once myself) and wandering far away from your heavenly Father's house. Come home, and leave your swine trough. Do not feed any longer on the husks of sensual delights. For the sake of Christ, arise and come

---

15. May God give each of us such passion.

home! Your heavenly Father now calls you. See yonder the best robe, even the righteousness of His dear Son, awaits you. See it, view it again and again. Consider at how dear a price it was purchased—even by the blood of God. Consider what great need you have of it. You are lost, undone, and damned forever without it. Come then, poor, guilty prodigals, come home. Indeed, I will not, like the elder brother in the Gospel, be angry; no, I will rejoice with the angels in heaven. And, oh, that God would now bow the heavens and come down! Descend, O Son of God, descend. As You have shown me such mercy, let Your blessed Spirit apply Your righteousness to some young prodigals now before You, and clothe their naked souls with Your best robe![16]

But I must speak a word to you, young maidens, as well as young men. I see many of you adorned as to your bodies, but are your souls naked? Which of you can say, "The Lord is my righteousness"? Which of you ever desired to be dressed in this robe of invaluable price, without which you are no better than whited sepulchers in the sight of God? (See Matthew 23:27.) Young maidens, do not forget any longer your chief and only ornament. Oh, seek for the Lord to be your righteousness, or otherwise burning will soon be upon you instead of beauty!

And what will I say to those of you of a middle age, you busy merchants, you cumbered Marthas, who, with all your gains, have not yet gotten the Lord to be your righteousness? Alas, what profit will there be of all your labor under the sun if you do not secure this pearl of invaluable price? (See Matthew 13:46.) This one thing, so absolutely needful that it alone can stand in your place when all other things are taken from you. Therefore, do not anxiously labor any longer for the meat that perishes, but from now on seek for the Lord to be your righteousness, a righteousness that will entitle you to life everlasting.

I see also many hoary heads here, and perhaps the most of them cannot say, "The Lord is my righteousness." O gray-headed sinner, I

---

16. Can't you see a passionate Whitefield lifting his tear-filled eyes up to heaven and openly pleading for God's mercy to be shown to those who stood before him? How far we have strayed from such preaching.

could weep over you! Your gray hairs, which ought to be your crown, and in which perhaps you glory, are now your shame. You do not know that the Lord is your righteousness. Oh, haste then, haste, aged sinners, and seek redeeming love! Alas, you have one foot already in the grave, your glass is just run out, your sun is just going down, and it will set and leave you in an eternal darkness unless the Lord is your righteousness! Flee then, oh, flee for your lives! Do not be afraid. All things are possible with God. If you come, though it be at the eleventh hour, Christ Jesus will by no means cast you out. Seek then for the Lord to be your righteousness, and beseech Him to let you know how it is that a man may be born again when he is old!

But I must not forget the lambs of the flock. To feed them was one of my Lord's last commands. I know He will be angry with me if I do not tell them that the Lord may be their righteousness and that of such is the kingdom of heaven. Come then, you little children, come to Christ; the Lord Christ will be your righteousness. Do not think that you are too young to be converted. Perhaps many of you may be nine or ten years old and yet cannot say, "The Lord is our righteousness," which many have said, though younger than you. Come then, while you are young. Perhaps you may not live to be old. Do not wait for other people. If your fathers and mothers will not come to Christ, come without them. Let children lead them, and show them how the Lord may be their righteousness. Our Lord Jesus Christ loved little children. You are His lambs; He bids me to feed you. I pray that God will make you willing to take the Lord for your righteousness.

Here, then, I could conclude. Oh, that you would seek the Lord to be your righteousness! Who knows but you may find Him? For in Jesus Christ there is neither male nor female, bond nor free (Galatians 3:28); even you may be the children of God, if you believe in Jesus. Did you never read of the eunuch belonging to the queen of Candace? He believed. The Lord was his righteousness. He was baptized. You must also believe, and you will be saved. Christ Jesus is the same now as He was yesterday, and He will wash you in His own blood. Go home, then, turn the words of the text into a prayer, and entreat the Lord to be your righteousness. *"Even so, come, Lord Jesus"* (Revelation 22:20). Come quickly into all our souls! Amen, Lord Jesus, amen and amen!

"Sinners in the Hands of an Angry God" is a sermon that would have a hard time finding a preacher courageous enough to utter its powerful words today. Jonathan Edwards opened his mouth boldly and preached the Gospel with passion.

He put his finger on the biblical reason for why every man and woman must come to Jesus or perish. This kind of straightforward and honest preaching was typical of Jonathan Edwards and was used by God to break hardened hearts. The preaching of the Law stripped proud sinners of their self-righteousness, left them naked and uncovered before a holy God, and softened their hearts to humbly receive the mercy of the Gospel.

—Kirk

JONATHAN EDWARDS

Jonathan Edwards was never a man to evade a problem, especially one that concerned the fate of a man's soul. Rather, he was one of the most honest expositors of his time. To this day, he is considered one of the greatest philosophers America has ever produced. His writings and sermons contain some of the most accessible words ever written or spoken on most of the major doctrines of Christianity.

Born in East Windsor, Connecticut, in 1703, Jonathan Edwards was the only son of the Reverend Timothy Edwards and Esther Stoddard Edwards. He was a dedicated student and scholar from his early youth, well before he entered Yale University at the age of thirteen. At Yale he was immersed not only in the most current thought coming out of Europe, but also in the debates between Calvinism and the more "liberal" movements that challenged it—such as Deism, Socinianism, Arianism, and especially Anglican Arminianism. In addition to his scholarly bent, Edwards was philosophical and had an appetite for the divine; his academics never took a higher place than his devotion to God. From early in his life, Edwards committed himself to vindicating his beliefs.

In 1729, after earning a master of divinity from Yale, Edwards succeeded his grandfather, the famed evangelist Solomon Stoddard, as full pastor of the First Church of Northampton, Massachusetts. In the twenty-four years that he lived in Northampton, Edwards was deeply concerned with the nature of true religion. Although only three or four generations had passed since the Puritans had come to the New World, the religious fervor of the church had more or less evaporated. Both thinking and living had fallen to a lower plane. In such an atmosphere, Edwards knew that sinners would never choose to serve and glorify God unless God changed their hearts and planted in them the desire to seek Him.

The widespread revivals of the early 1740s, known to historians as the "Great Awakening," stimulated one of the two most fruitful periods for Edwards' writings. Edwards became known for his emphasis on the sovereignty of God, the depravity of humankind, the reality of hell, and the necessity of a "New Birth" conversion. He gained international fame as a revivalist and "theologian of the heart" after publishing "A Faithful Narrative of the Surprising Work of God" (1738), which described the 1734–1735 awakening in his church and served as an empirical model for American and British revivalists alike.

Edwards died on March 22, 1758, following complications from a smallpox inoculation. He is buried in the Princeton Cemetery.

As Edwards recognized, true religion is a matter of the heart. Edwards was keenly aware of the fact that true religion has to be lived out, and he set forth to transform his congregation, as well as congregations throughout New England, from "mere believers who understood the logic of Christian doctrine to converted Christians who were genuinely moved by the principles of their belief."

SINNERS IN THE HANDS OF AN ANGRY GOD

Jonathan Edwards
Enfield, Connecticut
July 8, 1741

"Their foot shall slide in due time."
—Deuteronomy 32:35

THE STATE OF HUMANKIND

In this verse, the vengeance of God is threatened on the wicked, unbelieving Israelites, who were God's visible people and who lived under the means of grace, but who, notwithstanding all God's wonderful works toward them, remained *"void of counsel,"* having no understanding in them (Deuteronomy 32:28). Under all the cultivations of heaven, they brought forth bitter and poisonous fruit, as in two verses that precede our text:

> For their vine is of the vine of Sodom, and of the fields of Gomorrah:
> their grapes are grapes of gall, their clusters are bitter: their wine is
> the poison of dragons, and the cruel venom of asps.   (vv. 32–33)

The phrase I have chosen for my text, *"Their foot shall slide in due time,"* seems to imply the following things. Each of these four implications relates to the punishment and destruction to which these wicked Israelites were exposed.

First of all, the Israelites were always exposed to destruction, just as one who stands or walks in slippery places is always prone to a fall. This is implied in the manner in which their destruction was to come upon them, for it is represented by their foot sliding. The same idea is expressed in Psalm 73:18: *"Surely thou didst set them in slippery places: thou castedst them down into destruction."*

Second, the phrase implies that they were always exposed to sudden and unexpected destruction. The man who walks in slippery places is at every moment liable to fall. He cannot foresee whether he will stand one moment or fall the next; and when he does fall, he falls at once, without warning. This is also expressed in the Seventy-third Psalm:

Surely thou didst set them in slippery places: thou castedst them down into destruction. How are they brought into desolation, as in a moment! (vv. 18–19)

Another thing implied by the text is that they are liable to fall of themselves, without being thrown down by the hand of another. In the same way, one who stands or walks on slippery ground needs nothing but his own weight to throw him down.

Fourth, the reason why they have not fallen already and do not fall now is only that God's appointed time has not yet come. For it is written that, when that due time, or appointed time, comes, *"their foot shall slide."*

At that time, they will be left to fall, as they are inclined by their own weight. God will not hold them up in these slippery places any longer but will let them go. And then, at that very instant, they will fall into destruction, just as he who stands on such slippery, declining ground, on the edge of a pit, cannot stand alone; for when he is let go, he immediately falls and is lost.

From this, observe what our text means: There is nothing that keeps wicked men out of hell, at any one moment, except the mere pleasure of God.[17] By "the mere pleasure of God," I mean His sovereign pleasure, His all-powerful will, restrained by no obligation, hindered by no manner of difficulty; nothing else but God's sovereign will has a hand in the preservation of wicked men. The truth of this observation may become clear through the following considerations.

First, there is no lack of power in God to cast wicked men into hell at any moment. Men's hands cannot be strong when God rises up. The strongest have no power to resist Him, nor can any man escape from His hands. He is not only able to cast wicked men into hell, but He can also most easily do it.

Sometimes an earthly ruler finds it very difficult to subdue a rebel who has found means to fortify himself and has made himself strong by having great numbers of followers. However, it is not so with God. There is no fortress that is any defense from the power of God. Though hand join in hand, and vast multitudes of God's enemies combine and associate themselves, they are easily broken into pieces. They are as great heaps of chaff before the whirlwind (see Isaiah 17:13) or large quantities of dry stubble before devouring flames. (See Nahum 1:10.)

We find it easy to tread on and crush a worm that we see crawling on the ground. It is just as easy for us to cut or singe a slender thread by which something hangs. Now, think of how easy it is for God, whenever He pleases, to cast His enemies down to hell. Who are we that we should think we can stand before Him, at whose rebuke the earth trembles and before whom the rocks are thrown down? (See Nahum 1:4–6.)

The second consideration is that sinners deserve to be cast into hell. Divine justice never stands in the way of God's using His power at any

---

17. Nowadays the word *hell* is rarely used from a pulpit; this famous sermon makes reference to it forty-six times.

moment to destroy them; it makes no objection whatsoever. Rather, justice calls aloud for an infinite punishment of their sins. Divine justice says of the tree that brings forth fruit like that of the poisonous grapes of Sodom, *"Cut it down; why cumbereth it the ground?"* (Luke 13:7). The sword of divine justice is every moment brandished over their heads, and it is nothing but the hand of all-powerful mercy, and God's sovereign will, that holds it back.

Third, sinners are already under a sentence of condemnation to hell. They not only justly deserve to be cast down to that place, but the sentence of the Law of God[18]—that eternal and immutable rule of righteousness that God has fixed between Himself and humankind—has also gone out against them, and stands against them, so that they are already bound over to hell.

Consider what is written in the book of John: *"He that believeth not is condemned already"* (John 3:18). Every unconverted man properly belongs to hell; that is his place; his nature is from there. *"Ye are from beneath"* (John 8:23), said Christ. And the sinner is bound to that place, for hell is the place assigned to him by justice, by God's Word, and by the sentence of His unchangeable Law.

Fourth, let us consider that sinners are the objects of that very same anger and wrath of God that is expressed in the torments of hell. The reason that sinners do not go down to hell, at each moment, is not because God, in whose power they are, is not then very angry with them.

He is angry with many miserable creatures now tormented in hell, all of whom feel and bear the fierceness of His wrath there. Yet God is much angrier with great numbers of people who are now on earth. In

---

18. It is important to remember that this sermon was preached in an age when it was common practice to preach the thunderings of God's Law. If it is taken out of its historical context and preached from the pulpits of those who never expound the Ten Commandments, it will likely do more harm than good. Hellfire preaching without the Law of God to make judgment *reasonable* produces "converts" who lack contrition. They never understand the grace of the Cross—that we *deserved* hell, but God gave us heaven—because without the Law sin cannot be seen in its true light (Romans 7:7). They therefore lack the necessary gratitude for mercy, and gratitude is necessary before we can delight in God's will.

fact, He is angrier with many who are now in the congregations of our churches, many who seem to be at ease, than He is with many of those who are now in the flames of hell.

It is not because God is unmindful of their wickedness, and does not resent it, that He does not let loose His hand and cut them off. God is not altogether similar to these human beings, although they may imagine Him to be so. The wrath of God burns against them continually; their damnation does not slumber. The pit is prepared; the fire is made ready; the furnace is now hot, ready to receive them; the flames do now rage and glow. The glittering sword is sharpened and held over them, and the pit has opened its mouth under them.

Fifth, the devil stands ready to fall upon them and seize them as his own, at whatever moment God will permit him. Sinners belong to him; he has their souls in his possession and under his dominion. The Scripture represents them as his goods. (See Luke 11:21–22.) The devils watch them; they are always at the right hand of these wicked men; they stand waiting for them—like greedy, hungry lions that see their prey and expect to have it—but are for the present kept back.

Now, if God should withdraw His hand, by which the devils are restrained, they would in one moment fly upon those poor souls. The old serpent is gaping for them; hell opens its mouth wide to receive them; and if God should permit it, they would be hastily swallowed up and lost.

Sixth, consider that, in the souls of wicked men, hellish principles reign, which would immediately kindle and flame out into hellfire if it were not for God's restraints. There is laid, in the very nature of carnal men, a foundation for the torments of hell. Corrupt principles, reigning in power in them and in full possession of them, are seeds of hellfire.

These principles are active and powerful and are exceedingly violent in nature. If it were not for the restraining hand of God upon them, they would soon break out; they would flame out in the same manner that the same corruptions, and the same enmity, do in the hearts of damned souls, and they would beget the same torments as they do in those souls.

The souls of the wicked are, in Scripture, compared to the troubled sea: *"But the wicked are like the troubled sea, when it cannot rest, whose waters cast up mire and dirt"* (Isaiah 57:20). For the present, God restrains their wickedness by His mighty power, as He does the raging waves of the troubled sea, saying, *"Hitherto shalt thou come, but no further"* (Job 38:11); but if God should withdraw that restraining power, their wickedness would soon overwhelm them.

Sin is the ruin and misery of the soul. It is destructive in its nature; and if God should leave it without restraint, nothing else would be needed to make the soul perfectly miserable. The corruption of the heart of man is immoderate and boundless in its fury; and while wicked men live on this earth, it is like fire pent up by God's restraints. If it were let loose, it would set on fire the whole course of nature. Since the heart is now a cesspool of sin, if sin were not restrained, it would immediately turn the soul into a fiery oven or a furnace of fire and brimstone.

Seventh, it is no security to wicked men—not even for a moment—when they can see no visible means of death at hand. Natural man derives no security from the fact that he is healthy or that he cannot foresee the sudden way in which he will go out of the world. There is no comfort in finding no visible danger in any respect in his circumstances. The manifold and continual experience of the world, in all ages, shows this is no evidence; the world tries to prove that a man is not on the very brink of eternity, and that the next step will not be into another world, but to no avail.

The unseen, unthought-of ways and means by which people suddenly go out of the world are innumerable and inconceivable. Unconverted men walk over the pit of hell on a rotten covering, and there are countless places in this covering that are so weak that the covering will not bear their weight, and these places are not seen. The arrows of death fly unseen at midday; the sharpest sight cannot discern them.

God has so many different, unsearchable ways of taking wicked men out of the world and sending them to hell, that there is nothing to indicate that God has to go out of the ordinary course of His providence or perform a miracle in order to destroy any wicked man, at any moment. All the means by which sinners may go out of the world are so in God's hands, and so universally and absolutely subject to His power and determination, that the fate of sinners would not depend one bit less on the sovereign will of God if such means were never made use of or never had any bearing on the case.

Our eighth consideration is that natural man's prudence and care to preserve his own life, or the care of others to preserve him, do not secure him for a moment. Divine providence and universal experience bear testimony to this. Man's own wisdom does not secure him from death; if it were otherwise, we would see some difference between the wise and shrewd men of the world, and others. Perhaps wise men would have less liability to early and unexpected death. But, how is it, in fact? *"How dieth the wise man? [Even] as the fool"* (Ecclesiastes 2:16).

The ninth thing is that all wicked men's pains and contrivances, which they use to escape hell while they continue to reject Christ and so remain wicked men, do not secure them from hell for even one moment. Almost every natural man who hears of hell flatters himself that he will escape it.[19] He depends on himself for his own security; he flatters himself because of what he has done, what he is now doing, or what he intends to do.

Everyone lays out in his own mind how he will avoid damnation and flatters himself that he contrives well for himself and that his schemes will not fail. He may indeed hear that there are few who are saved, and that the greater part of men who have died before him have gone to

___

19. One can often reason with the unregenerate to a point where they will admit that God should punish the perpetrators of heinous crimes. It makes sense, for example, that if God is good, He should bring retribution to a man who has viciously raped and murdered a young girl. Yet the unregenerate person mistakenly thinks that God's standards are so low that He will restrict His judgment to what humankind considers to be serious crimes. However, God is so good that all sin is serious to Him.

hell; but each one imagines that he lays out matters for his own escape better than others have done. He does not intend to go to that place of torment; he says within himself that he intends to take effectual care and to order matters for himself so as not to fail.

Even so, the foolish children of men miserably delude themselves in their own schemes, being far too confident in their own strength and wisdom; they trust in nothing but shadows. The greater part of those who, up to the present time, have lived under the same means of grace, and are now dead, have undoubtedly gone to hell. This was not because they were not as wise as those who are now alive; nor was it because they did not lay out matters as well for themselves to secure their own escape.

If we could speak with them and inquire of them, one by one, whether they, when they were alive and when they used to hear about hell, ever expected to be the subjects of misery, we doubtless would hear them reply, "No, I never intended to come here. I had laid out matters otherwise in my mind; I thought I had contrived well for myself; I thought my scheme had been good. I intended to take effectual care, but death came upon me unexpectedly. I did not look for it at that time, or in that manner; it came as a thief. Death outwitted me; God's wrath was too quick for me. Oh, my cursed foolishness! I was flattering myself and pleasing myself with vain dreams of what I would do hereafter; and when I was saying, 'Peace and safety,' then sudden destruction came upon me." (See 1 Thessalonians 5:3.)

God has placed Himself under no obligation, by any promise, to keep any natural man out of hell. God certainly has made no promises, either of eternal life or of any deliverance or preservation from eternal death, except those that are contained in the covenant of grace, the promises that are given in Christ, in whom all the promises are yea and amen. (See 2 Corinthians 1:20.) But, surely, they who are not the children of the covenant, who do not believe in any of the promises, and who have no interest in the Mediator of the covenant, have no interest in the promises of the covenant of grace.

Consequently, whatever some people have imagined and pretended to understand about the promises made to natural men's earnest seeking and knocking, it is clear and manifest that, whatever pains a natural man takes in religion, whatever prayers he makes, until he believes in Christ, God is under no manner of obligation to keep him from eternal destruction for even a moment.

Thus it is that natural men are held in the hand of God, over the pit of hell; they have deserved the fiery pit and are already sentenced to it; and God is dreadfully provoked. His anger is as great toward them as it is toward those who are actually suffering the executions and fierceness of His wrath in hell. These natural men have done nothing at all to appease or abate that anger, and God is not in the least bound by any promise to hold them up.

The devil is waiting for them; hell is gaping for them; the flames gather and flash about them and would prefer to lay hold of them and swallow them up. The fire pent up in their own hearts is struggling to break out, and they have no interest in any Mediator. There are no means within reach that can be any security to them. In short, they have no refuge, nothing to take hold of. All that preserves them every moment is the sovereign, all-powerful will, the uncovenanted, unobliged forbearance, of an incensed God.

APPLICATION: SINNER, BEWARE!

Now, what significance does this have to our daily lives? Perhaps this awful subject may awaken those who remain unconverted in the church, for what you have read is the case of everyone who is out of Christ.

If you are not a child of God, that world of misery, that lake of burning brimstone, is extended abroad under you. Below you is the dreadful pit of the glowing flames of the wrath of God; hell's mouth is gaping wide open, and you have nothing to stand upon, nor anything to take hold of. There is nothing between you and hell except the air; it is only the power and mere pleasure of God that holds you up.

You probably are not aware of this, for although you find you are kept out of hell, you do not see the hand of God in it. Instead, you attribute your current state to other things, such as the health of your body, your care of your own life, and the means you use for your own preservation. But, indeed, these things are nothing; if God should withdraw His hand, they would avail no more to keep you from falling than the thin air can hold up a person who is suspended in it.

Your wickedness makes you as heavy as lead; it drives you down, with great weight and pressure, toward hell. And if God were to let you go, you would immediately sink and swiftly descend and plunge into the bottomless gulf. At that moment, you will see that your health, your own care and prudence, your best contrivance, and all your righteousness, have no more influence to uphold you and keep you out of hell than a spider's web has to stop a falling rock.

Were it not for the sovereign pleasure of God, the earth would not bear you for one moment, for you are a burden to it. The creation groans with you: *"For we know that the whole creation groaneth and travaileth in pain together"* (Romans 8:22); creation is unwillingly made subject to the bondage of your corruption.

The sun does not willingly shine upon you to give you light to serve sin and Satan. The earth does not willingly yield her increase to satisfy your lusts, nor is it willingly a stage for your wickedness to be acted upon. The air does not willingly give you breath to maintain the flame of life in your vitals while you spend your life in the service of God's enemies.

God's creation is good, and was made for men to serve God with; it does not willingly serve as an instrument to any other purpose. In fact, it groans when it is abused for purposes so directly contrary to its nature and end. The world would spew you out were it not for the sovereign hand of God.

> *For the creature was made subject to vanity, not willingly, but by reason of him who hath subjected the same in hope, because the creature itself also shall be delivered from the bondage of corruption into the glorious liberty of the children of God.* (Romans 8:20–21)

The black clouds of God's wrath, full of the dreadful storm and big with thunder, now hang directly over your head; and were it not for the restraining hand of God, His wrath would immediately burst forth upon you. The sovereign pleasure of God, for the present, stays His rough wind; otherwise, it would come with fury, and your destruction would come like a whirlwind, and you would be like the chaff of the summer threshing floor.

The wrath of God is like great waters that are dammed for the present; they increase more and more, and rise higher and higher, until an outlet is given. The longer the stream is stopped, the more rapid and mighty is its course when at last it is let loose. It is true that judgment against your evil works has not yet been executed; the floods of God's vengeance have been withheld. Nevertheless, your guilt, in the meantime, is constantly increasing, and you are every day storing up more wrath for yourself. (See Romans 2:5.)

The waters are constantly rising and waxing mightier and mightier; and there is nothing but the mere pleasure of God to hold back the waters that press hard to go forward and are unwilling to be stopped. If God were only to withdraw His hand from the floodgate, it would immediately fly open, and the fiery floods of the fierceness and wrath of God would rush forth with inconceivable fury and would come upon you with omnipotent power. Think of it! If your strength were ten thousand times greater than it is—if it were ten thousand times greater than the strength of the stoutest, sturdiest devil in hell—it would be nothing to withstand or endure the wrath of God.

The bow of God's wrath is bent; the arrow is made ready on the string; and justice bends the arrow at your heart and strains the bow. It is nothing but the mere pleasure of God, and that of an angry God, without any promise or obligation at all, that keeps the arrow from being made drunk with your blood at every moment.

Therefore, you who have never passed under a great change of heart by the mighty power of the Spirit of God upon your soul; you who have never been born again and been made a new creature (see 2 Corinthians 5:17) and been raised from being dead in sin to a state of newness and previously unexperienced light and life, are in the hands of an angry God.

In whatever way you may have reformed your life in many respects and may have had religious inclinations and may have kept up a form of religion in your family, your prayer closet, and the house of God, it is nothing but God's mere pleasure that keeps you from being this moment swallowed up into everlasting destruction. However unconvinced you may now be of the truth of what you read, perhaps, later on, you will be fully convinced of it.

Note that it was the same for those who have already gone from this world; for destruction came suddenly upon most of them when they expected nothing of it and while they were saying, *"Peace and safety"* (1 Thessalonians 5:3). They see now that those things on which they depended for peace and safety were nothing but thin air and empty shadows.

The God who holds you over the pit of hell, as one might hold a spider or some loathsome insect over the fire, abhors you and is dreadfully provoked. His wrath toward you burns like fire; He looks upon you as worthy of nothing else but to be cast into the fire. His eyes are so pure that He cannot bear to have you in His sight; you are ten thousand times more abominable in His eyes than the most hateful, venomous serpent is in ours.[20]

You have offended Him infinitely more than ever a stubborn rebel did his prince; and yet it is nothing but His hand that holds you from falling into the fire every moment. There is no other reason to be given why you did not go to hell the moment you walked into the house of God on a Sunday morning, provoking His pure eyes by your sinful, wicked manner of attending His solemn worship.

There is no other reason why you did not go to hell last night, or why you were permitted to wake up again in this world after you had closed your eyes to sleep. And there is no other reason to be given why you have not dropped into hell since you woke up this morning, except that God's hand has held you up. Indeed, there is nothing else that can stand as a reason why you do not this very moment drop down into hell.

O sinner! Consider the fearful danger you are in! It is a great furnace of wrath, a wide and bottomless pit, full of the fire of wrath, over which you are held by the hand of God. And this is the God whose wrath is provoked and incensed as much against you as against many of the damned in hell. You hang by a slender thread, with the flames of divine wrath flashing about it and ready every moment to singe it and burn it asunder; yet you have no interest in any Mediator, and nothing to lay hold of to save yourself, nothing to keep off the flames of wrath, nothing of your own, nothing that you ever have done, nothing that you can do, to induce God to spare you for even a moment.

A WARNING TO ALL

What I have written thus far is not directed only toward those men whom we would look upon and consider as wicked. Rather, my words

20. This is a little different from the ever popular "God loves you and has a wonderful plan for your life." Although God is a merciful God, we cannot expect Him to overlook our sin. God is holy and just, which means there is a price for our sins. Isn't it wonderful that the grace of God sent Jesus to fulfill the Law in our place?

should serve as a warning to everyone—every man, every woman, and every child. Because all are born into sin, we must take into consideration the following.

The wrath of kings is very much dreaded, especially that of absolute monarchs, who have the possessions and lives of their subjects wholly in their power, to be disposed of at their mere will. The Scriptures attest to the terribleness of such wrath:

> *The fear of a king is as the roaring of a lion: whoso provoketh him to anger sinneth against his own soul.* (Proverbs 20:2)

However, the wrath that is held against us is the wrath of the infinite God. If it were only the wrath of a man, though he were the most potent ruler of the world, it would be little in comparison.

Anyone who greatly enrages a ruler of this world is liable to undergo the most extreme torments that human cleverness can invent or that human power can inflict. Even so, the greatest earthly sovereigns, in their greatest majesty and strength and when clothed in their greatest terrors, are but feeble, despicable worms of the dust in comparison with the great and almighty Creator and King of heaven and earth.

All the kings of the earth, before God, are as grasshoppers (see Isaiah 40:22): They can do very little, even when they are most enraged and when they have exerted the utmost of their fury. They are nothing, and less than nothing, in comparison with God. Both their love and their hatred are to be despised. The wrath of the great King of Kings is much more terrible than theirs, just as His majesty is greater than theirs.

> *And I say unto you my friends, Be not afraid of them that kill the body, and after that have no more that they can do. But I will forewarn you whom ye shall fear: Fear him, which after he hath killed*

hath power to cast into hell; yea, I say unto you, Fear him.

(Luke 12:4–5)

Second, it is the fierceness of His wrath that you are exposed to, as you have sinned against God. We often read of the fury of God, as in Isaiah 59:18: *"According to their deeds, accordingly he will repay, fury to his adversaries."* The same idea is expressed in Isaiah 66:15:

> For, behold, the LORD will come with fire, and with his chariots like a whirlwind, to render his anger with fury, and his rebuke with flames of fire.

We see this in many other places in the Scriptures. In Revelation 19:15 we read of *"the winepress of the fierceness and wrath of Almighty God."* The words are exceptionally terrible. If only the words "the wrath of God" had been written, it would have implied that which is infinitely dreadful. But it is *"the fierceness and wrath of Almighty God."* The fury of God! The fierceness of Jehovah! Oh, how dreadful that must be! Who can utter or imagine what such expressions carry in them?

Let us examine this verse further. It reads, *"the fierceness and wrath of **Almighty** God,"* as though there would be a very great manifestation of His almighty power in what the fierceness of His wrath would inflict, as though omnipotence would be enraged and exerted, just as men are inclined to exert their strength in the fierceness of their wrath.

What will the consequence be? What will become of the poor worms that will suffer under it? Whose hands can be strong? And whose heart can endure? (See Ezekiel 22:14.) To what a dreadful, inexpressible, inconceivable depth of misery must the poor creature be sunk who becomes the victim of this wrath!

You who remain in an unregenerate state, consider this: The fact that God will execute the fierceness of His anger implies that He will inflict wrath without any pity. When God beholds the unspeakable extremity of your condition and sees your torment to be so vastly dis-proportional to your strength and how your poor soul is crushed and sinks down, as it were, into an infinite gloom, He will have no compassion upon you; He will not hold back the executions of His wrath or in the least lighten His hand.

There will be no moderation or mercy, nor will God then at all stay His rough wind. (See Isaiah 27:8.) He will have no regard for your welfare, nor will He be at all concerned about your increasing suffering, except that you will not suffer beyond what strict justice requires. Nothing will be withheld with the reason that it is too hard for you to bear.

> *Therefore will I also deal in fury: mine eye shall not spare, neither will I have pity: and though they cry in mine ears with a loud voice, yet will I not hear them.* (Ezekiel 8:18)

Now God stands ready to pity you; this is a day of mercy; you may cry now with some encouragement of obtaining mercy. But once the day of mercy is past, your most lamentable and miserable cries and shrieks will be in vain; you will be wholly lost and thrown away, and there will be no regard for your welfare.

God will have no other use to put you to, except to suffer misery; you will be allowed to exist for no other end. You will be a vessel of wrath, *"fitted to destruction"* (Romans 9:22),[21] and there will be no other use for this vessel, except to be filled full of wrath. God will be so far from pitying you when you cry to Him that He will only laugh at you.

Note what He says in the following passage:

> *Because I have called, and ye refused; I have stretched out my hand, and no man regarded; but ye have set at nought all my counsel,*

21. The frightening thing about this sermon is that it is grounded in Holy Scripture. We should be horrified beyond words at the fate of the ungodly and earnestly plead with them to flee from the wrath to come.

and would none of my reproof: I also will laugh at your calamity; I will mock when your fear cometh; when your fear cometh as deso-lation, and your destruction cometh as a whirlwind; when distress and anguish cometh upon you. Then shall they call upon me, but I will not answer; they shall seek me early, but they shall not find me: for that they hated knowledge, and did not choose the fear of the Lord: *they would none of my counsel: they despised all my reproof. Therefore shall they eat of the fruit of their own way, and be filled with their own devices. For the turning away of the simple shall slay them, and the prosperity of fools shall destroy them. But whoso hear-keneth unto me shall dwell safely, and shall be quiet from fear of evil.* (Proverbs 1:24–33)

How awful are those words, also, from Isaiah 63:3, which are the words of the great God:

I will tread them in mine anger, and trample them in my fury; and their blood shall be sprinkled upon my garments, and I will stain all my raiment.

It is, perhaps, impossible to imagine words that carry in them greater manifestations of these three things: contempt, hatred, and fierceness of indignation. If you cry to God to pity you, He will be so far from pitying you in your downcast state or from showing you the least regard or favor that, instead of that, He will only tread you underfoot. And although He will know that you cannot bear the weight of omnipotence treading upon you, He will not regard that, but He will crush you under His feet without mercy.

Indeed, He will crush out your blood and make it fly, and it will be sprinkled on His garments so as to stain all His clothing. He will not only hate you, but He will also hold you in the utmost contempt: No place will be thought fit for you except under His feet, to be trodden down as the mire of the streets.

Third, the misery to which you are exposed is that which God will inflict for the very purpose of showing what that wrath of Jehovah is. God has had it on His heart to show to angels and men not only how excellent His love is, but also how terrible His wrath is.

Sometimes earthly kings have a mind to show how terrible their wrath is by the extreme punishments they execute on those who provoke them. Nebuchadnezzar, that mighty and haughty monarch of the Chaldean empire, was willing to show his wrath when he was enraged with Shadrach, Meshach, and Abednego. (See Daniel 3.) Accordingly, he gave orders that the burning fiery furnace should be heated seven times hotter than it ever was before (see verse 19); doubtless, it was raised to the utmost degree of fierceness that human ingenuity could raise it.

Like Nebuchadnezzar, the great God is also willing to show His wrath and to magnify His awful majesty and mighty power in the extreme sufferings of His enemies. Notice what is written in Romans 9:22:

What if God, willing to show his wrath, and to make his power known, endured with much longsuffering the vessels of wrath fitted to destruction?

And, seeing that this is what He has determined—even to show how terrible the unrestrained wrath, the fury, and the fierceness of Jehovah is—He will carry it out to its fulfillment.

This will be something accomplished and brought to pass that will be dreadful to any witness of it. When the great and angry God has risen up and executed His awful vengeance on a poor sinner, and the wretch is actually suffering the infinite weight and power of His indignation, then God will call upon the whole universe to behold the awful majesty and mighty power that is to be seen in it.

And the people shall be as the burnings of lime: as thorns cut up shall they be burned in the fire. Hear, ye that are far off, what I have done; and, ye that are near, acknowledge my might. The sinners in Zion are afraid; fearfulness hath surprised the hypocrites.

(Isaiah 33:12–14)

It will be the same with you who are in an unconverted state if you continue in it. The infinite might and majesty and terribleness of the omnipotent God will be magnified upon you in the unspeakable intensity of your torments. You will be tormented in the presence of the holy angels and in the presence of the Lamb; and when you are in this state of suffering, the glorious inhabitants of heaven will go forth and look on the awful spectacle that they may see what the wrath and fierceness of the Almighty is. Then, when they have seen it, they will fall down and adore that great power and majesty.

Read from the Scriptures in Isaiah 66:23–24:

And it shall come to pass, that from one new moon to another, and from one sabbath to another, shall all flesh come to worship before me, saith the LORD. And they shall go forth, and look upon the carcases of the men that have transgressed against me: for their worm shall not die, neither shall their fire be quenched; and they shall be an abhorring unto all flesh.

Certainly this is worth your consideration, even now, for *"all have sinned, and come short of the glory of God"* (Romans 3:23).

The fourth thing you must consider is that the wrath of God is an everlasting wrath. It would be dreadful to suffer this *"fierceness and wrath of Almighty God"* (Revelation 19:15) for just one moment, but you must suffer it for all eternity. There will be no end to this exquisitely horrible misery. When you look forward, you will see a long forever, a boundless duration before you, which will swallow up your thoughts and amaze your soul; and you will absolutely lose all hope or confidence of ever having any deliverance, any end, any mitigation, any rest at all.

You will know without question that you must wear out long ages, millions and millions of ages, in wrestling and conflicting with this almighty, merciless vengeance. And then, when you have done so, when so many ages have actually been spent by you in this manner, you will know that everything you have suffered is but a pinpoint compared to what remains. Your punishment will indeed be infinite.

Oh, who can express the state of a soul in such circumstances! All that we can possibly say about it gives but a very feeble, faint representation of it; it is inexpressible and inconceivable, for *"who knoweth the power of* [God's] *anger"* (Psalm 90:11)?

How dreadful is the state of those who are daily and hourly in danger of this great wrath and infinite misery! Nevertheless, this is the dismal case of all souls hearing this who have not been born again, however moral and strict, sober and religious, they may otherwise be. Oh, that you would consider it, whether you are young or old!

There is reason to think that there are many now hearing this, who will actually be the subjects of this very misery for all eternity. I do not know who they are, or in what places they now sit, or what thoughts they now have. It may be that they are now at ease and take in all these things without much disturbance and are now flattering themselves that they are not the people in great jeopardy, promising themselves that they will escape.

If we knew that there was one person, and only one, among all our friends and neighbors, who was to be the subject of this misery, what an awful thing it would be to think of! If we knew who it was, what an awful sight it would be to see such a person! How all the rest of our friends and neighbors would lift up a lamentable and bitter cry over him!

But, alas! instead of one, how many are likely to remember receiving this message once they are in hell? It would be no great wonder to me if some who hear this should be in hell in a very short time, even before this year is out. And it would be no wonder if some people, who now sit in health, quiet and secure, should be there before tomorrow morning. And, finally, those of you who continue in a natural condition, who will keep out of hell longest, will be there in just a little time! Your damnation does not slumber; it will come swiftly and, in all probability, very suddenly upon many of you. You have reason to marvel that you are not already in hell.

This, doubtless, has been the case of some people whom you have seen and known, who never deserved hell more than you and who had every reason to believe they would be alive today, just as you are. Their case is past all hope; they are crying in extreme misery and perfect despair. But you are in the land of the living, and you have an opportunity to obtain salvation. What would those poor, damned, hopeless souls not give for one day's opportunity such as you now enjoy?

And now, you have an extraordinary opportunity, a day wherein Christ has thrown the door of mercy wide open and stands calling and crying with a loud voice to poor sinners; a day wherein many are flocking to Him, and pressing into the kingdom of God. Many are daily coming from the east, west, north, and south. Many who were very recently in the same miserable condition that you are in, are now in a happy state, with their hearts filled with love for Him who has loved them and washed them from their sins in His own blood; they are rejoicing *"in* [the] *hope of the glory of God"* (Romans 5:2).

How awful it is to be left behind on such a day! How horrible to see so many others feasting while you are pining and perishing! How dreadful to see so many rejoicing and singing for joy of heart while you have cause to mourn for sorrow of heart and to howl for vexation of spirit! How can you rest one moment in such a condition? Are your souls not as precious as the souls of the people who are flocking to Christ every day?

Do you not know many people who have lived long in the world and are not, even to this day, born again? They are *"aliens from the commonwealth of Israel"* (Ephesians 2:12) and have done nothing, ever since they were born, except treasure up *"wrath against the day of wrath,"* just as the apostle wrote in Romans 2:5:

> But after thy hardness and impenitent heart treasurest up unto thyself wrath against the day of wrath and revelation of the righteous judgment of God.

O my friends, if you have not yet turned to Christ, even in your later years, then your case is extremely dangerous. Your guilt and hardness of heart are extremely great. Do you not see how people of your years are generally passed over and left, in the remarkable and wonderful dispensation of God's mercy? You must carefully consider your condition and awaken thoroughly out of sleep. You cannot bear the fierceness and wrath of the infinite God.

And you, young men and young women, will you neglect this precious season that you now enjoy, when so many others of your age are renouncing all youthful vanities and flocking to Christ? You, especially now, have an extraordinary opportunity; but if you neglect it, it will soon be with you as it was with those who spent all the precious days of youth in sin and are now in such a dreadful state of blindness and hardness.

And you, children who are unconverted, do you not know that you are going down to hell, to bear the dreadful wrath of that God who is now angry with you every day and every night? Will you be content to be the children of the devil when so many other children in the world have been converted and are the holy and happy children of the King of Kings?

Let all who are yet out of Christ and hanging over the pit of hell—whether they be old men and women, or middle-aged, or young people, or little children—now hearken to the loud calls of God's Word and His providence. This acceptable year of the Lord, a day of such great favor to some, will doubtless be a day of as remarkable vengeance to others.

Men's hearts harden, and their guilt increases rapidly, in times such as these if they neglect their souls; and never has there been so great a danger of such people being given up to hardness of heart and blindness of mind. God seems now to be hastily gathering in His elect in all parts of the world.

Most likely, the greater part of adults who will ever be saved will be brought in now in a short period of time, and it will be as it was during the great outpouring of the Spirit upon the Jews in the apostles' days. The elect will obtain His Spirit, and the rest will be blinded. If this should be the case with you, you will eternally curse this day and will curse the day that ever you were born, to see such a season of the pouring out of God's Spirit. You will wish that you had died and gone to hell before you had seen it.

Now, undoubtedly, it is as it was in the days of John the Baptist:

The ax is laid unto the root of the trees: therefore every tree which bringeth not forth good fruit is hewn down, and cast into the fire.
(Matthew 3:10)

Therefore, let everyone who is out of Christ now awaken and fly from the wrath to come. The wrath of almighty God is now undoubtedly hanging over a great number of you. Let everyone fly out of Sodom:

Escape for thy life; look not behind thee, neither stay thou in all the plain; escape to the mountain, lest thou be consumed.
(Genesis 19:17)

Martin Luther came before Wesley, Whitefield, Spurgeon, and Edwards and opened the door for the entire Protestant movement. He was a revolutionary and a reformer. He exposed hypocrisy within the church and lived to bring the truth of the Scriptures to the common people. He coined the classic phrases *sola scriptura* and *sola fide*, meaning "Scripture alone" and "faith alone," respectively. This man suffered incredible persecution from the religious "elite" and thrived under the pressure—the usual results in the life of a man transformed by the living God.

—Kirk

MARTIN LUTHER

Martin Luther was born on November 10, 1483, in Eisleben, Germany, the son of Hans Luther, who worked in the copper mines, and Margarethe. He went to Latin school at Magdeburg and Eisenach and entered the University of Erfurt in 1501, graduating with a B.A. in 1502 and an M.A. in 1505. His father desired for him to be a lawyer, but Luther was drawn to the study of the Scriptures. In 1505, he made a decision that changed the course of his life: He decided to enter the Augustinian monastery at Erfurt. In 1507, he was ordained and went to the University of Wittenberg, where he lectured on philosophy and the Scriptures, becoming a powerful and influential preacher.

On a trip to Rome in 1510–11, he was appalled by the corruption he found there. Money was greatly needed at the time for the rebuilding of St. Peter's, and papal emissaries sought everywhere to raise funds by the sale of indulgences. When a person purchased an indulgence, it would "buy" him forgiveness for sin. The system was grossly abused, and Luther's indignation at the shameless traffic, carried on in particular by the Dominican Johann Tetzel, became irrepressible. As a professor of biblical exegesis at Wittenberg (1512–46), Luther was well-equipped with scriptural knowledge to challenge the abusers, and he immediately sought out God for guidance and direction. Luther's negative encounters with the ecclesiastical means of grace worked to both increase his criticism of the deplorable state of affairs within the church and, above all, to prompt his fundamental reconsideration of medieval theology. This reevaluation eventually culminated in the Reformation of the church.

Luther began to preach the doctrine of salvation by faith rather than by works. On October 31, 1517, he drew up his famous "Ninety-five Theses," which denied that the pope had any right to forgive sins, and nailed them to the church door at Wittenberg. His theses did not result in the desired discussion but rather led to a court of inquisition, culminating in Luther's excommunication after the Imperial Diet of Worms in 1521.

In order to protect Luther's life, Friedrich the Wise organized a "kidnapping," which Luther was aware of ahead of time. Luther spent a year on Friedrich's estates under the guise of Knight George of Wartburg. While there, he translated the New Testament into German. With his translation of the Bible into German, Martin Luther attained permanent fame for unifying the German language. His Bible became a standard for grammar and spelling.

After Luther's excommunication, he still lived a monklike life. His final break with his vows came when Luther married Katherine von Bora, a nun who had withdrawn from convent life, in June 1525. As they set up their household, the Protestant parish house was been born. After the Peasants' War in 1525, which Luther disapproved of, he promoted the development of the Protestant church through visitations and development of new church policies.

Luther died in Eisleben, the town of his birth, on February 18, 1546, and was buried in the Castle Church at Wittenberg.

THE LAW, FAITH, AND LOVE TO YOUR NEIGHBOR

Martin Luther
Preached by Luther in 1522 at Borna

"Then the same day at evening, being the first day of the week,
when the doors were shut where the disciples were assembled for
fear of the Jews, came Jesus and stood in the midst, and saith unto
them, Peace be unto you. And when he had so said, he showed unto
them his hands and his side. Then were the disciples glad, when
they saw the Lord. Then said Jesus to them again, Peace be unto
you: as my Father hath sent me, even so send I you. And when he
had said this, he breathed on them, and saith unto them, Receive
ye the Holy Ghost: whose soever sins ye remit, they are remitted
unto them; and whose soever sins ye retain, they are retained. But
Thomas, one of the twelve, called Didymus, was not with them
when Jesus came. The other disciples therefore said unto him, We
have seen the Lord. But he said unto them, Except I shall see in
his hands the print of the nails, and put my finger into the print
of the nails, and thrust my hand into his side, I will not believe.
And after eight days again his disciples were within, and Thomas
with them: then came Jesus, the doors being shut, and stood in
the midst, and said, Peace be unto you. Then saith he to Thomas,
Reach hither thy finger, and behold my hands; and reach hither thy
hand, and thrust it into my side: and be not faithless, but believing.
And Thomas answered and said unto him, My Lord and my God.
Jesus saith unto him, Thomas, because thou hast seen me, thou hast

*believed: blessed are they that have not seen, and yet have believed.
And many other signs truly did Jesus in the presence of his disciples, which are not written in this book: but these are written, that
ye might believe that Jesus is the Christ, the Son of God; and that
believing ye might have life through his name."*
—John 20:19–31

OF TRUE GODLINESS, THE LAW, AND FAITH

In today's Gospel, the life of a Christian and the two parts it consists of
are presented to us. First, the Lord shows Thomas His hands and feet.
Second, he is sent as Christ is sent. This is nothing other than faith and
love, the two thoughts that are preached to us in all the Gospel texts.

Formerly you heard, and, alas, it is preached throughout the world,
that if anyone desires to become righteous, he must begin with human
laws. This was done under the reign of Pope Leo X, and nearly all the
very best preachers preached nothing else except about how one is to be
outwardly pious and about good works that glitter before the world. But
this is still far from the true righteousness that avails before God.

There is another way to begin to become righteous that commences
by teaching us the Laws of God, from which we learn to know ourselves, what we are, and how impossible it is for us to fulfill the divine
Commandments. The Law speaks thus, "You shall have one God, worship Him alone, trust in Him alone, and seek help and comfort from
Him alone." (See Exodus 20:3–6.)[22] The heart hears this, and yet it

---

22. "The First Commandment of the Law demands that we have one God and honor Him—
that is, trust and confide in Him, build upon Him. This is true faith, by which we are made
children of God. Thus, the Law clearly reveals the sin of the Cain-like—their unbelief. In
like manner, you experience whether you believe or not. Without such a Law, no one could
experience or know this. Note, this is what Paul called a knowledge of sin by the Law."
Martin Luther

cannot do it. Why, then, does the Law command such an impossible thing? As I have said, it is to show us our inability, so we may learn to know ourselves and to see ourselves as we are, even as one sees himself in a mirror. When the conscience, smitten by God's Law, begins to quake and finds that it does not keep God's Commandments, then the Law does its proper work; for the true mission of the Law is only to terrify the conscience.

There are two classes of men who fulfill the Law, or who imagine they fulfill it. The first are those who, when they have heard it, begin with outward works. They desire to perform and fulfill it by works. How do they proceed? They say, "God has commanded you shall have one God. Surely I will worship no other God. I will serve Him and no idol and will have no heathen idolatrous image in my house or in my church. Why would I do this?" Such people make a show with their glittering, fabricated service of God, like the clergy in our day, and they think they keep this Law when they bend their knees and are able to sing and brag much about God. By this show, the poor laity also are deceived. They follow after the priests and also desire to obey the Law by their works. But the blind guides the blind and both fall into a pit (Luke 6:39). This is the first class—those who imagine they will keep the Law and yet do not.

The other class are those who know themselves by the Law and study what it seeks and requires. For instance, when the Law says, "You shall have one God and worship and honor Him alone," this heart meditates, "What does this mean? Should I bend my knees? What does it mean to have one God? It surely is something else than a bodily, outward reverence." Finally, this group realizes that the commandment is a very different thing than is generally supposed, that it is nothing except having trust and hope in God that He will help and assist in all anxiety and distress, in every temptation and adversity; that He will save man from sin, from death, from hell, and from the devil; and that without His help and salvation, man alone can do nothing. And this is the meaning of having one God. A heart, so thoroughly humble—namely, a heart that has become quite terrified and shaken by this commandment—desires to have God and, in its anxiety and trouble, flees to God alone.

Now, the hypocrites and work-saints, who lead a fine life before the world, are not able to do this, for their confidence is based upon their own righteousness and outward piety alone. Therefore, when God attacks them with the Law and causes the poor people to see that they have not kept the Law—no, not even the least of it—and when they are overwhelmed by anxiety and distress and an evil conscience, and when they perceive that external works will not suffice and that keeping the commandments of God is a very different thing from what they thought, then they rush ahead and seek ever more and more and other and still other works, and fancy that they will thereby quiet their consciences; but they greatly miss the right way. Hence, it comes to pass that one wishes to do it by rosaries, another by fasting; this one by prayer and that one by torturing his body; one runs to Rome, another to Jerusalem; here one becomes a monk, another a nun; and they seek their end in so many ways that they can scarcely be enumerated.

Why do they do all this? Because they wish to save themselves, to rescue and help themselves. The consequence of this is great blasphemy against God, for they also boast mightily of their works and brag, saying, "I have been in an order so long, I have prayed so many rosaries, have fasted so much, have done this and that; God will give me heaven as a reward." These actions are what it means to have an idol. This also is what Isaiah meant when he said, *"They worship the work of their own hands"* (Isaiah 2:8). He was not speaking of stone and wood but of the external works, which appear good and beautiful before men. These hypocrites are ingenious enough to give the chaff to God and to keep the wheat for themselves. This, then, is true idolatry, as Paul wrote to the Romans: *"Thou that abhorrest idols, dost thou commit sacrilege?"* (Romans 2:22). This is spiritual robbery.

Therefore, you will find that there is nothing good in any man of himself. But there is a distinction between this and the attitude of the upright, in whom the Law has exercised its work. The upright, when they feel their sickness and weakness, say, "God will help me. I trust in Him. I build upon Him. He is my rock and hope." But when trial, distress, and anxiety are at hand, the others lament and say, "Oh, where will I go?" They must at last despair of God, of themselves, and of their works, even if they have many of them.

These in the first group are false and unrighteous pupils of the Law, who presume to fulfill it by their works. For they have an appearance and glitter outwardly, but in their hearts they have nothing but filth and uncleanness. Therefore, they also merit nothing before God, who does not regard external works that are done without any heart in them.

Those in the second place are the true and real pupils who keep the Law, who know and are conscious that they do evil, and make nothing of themselves, surrender themselves, count all their works unclean in the eyes of God, and despair of themselves and all their own works. Those who do this will have no trouble, except that they must not deceive themselves with vain, fruitless thoughts and defer this matter until death; for if anyone persistently postpones this until death, he will have a sad future.

But we must take heed so that we will not despair, even if we still feel sinful inclinations and are not as pure as we would like to be. We will not entirely sweep all this rubbish out of our hearts because we are still flesh and blood. This much can surely be done: Outward wicked deeds can be prevented, and carnal, shameful words and works can be avoided, although it is attained with difficulty. But in this world it will never come to pass that you are free from lust and evil inclination. St. Jerome undertook to root such inclinations out of his heart by prayer, fasting, work, and torture of the body, but he found out that what he accomplished was of no avail; the desire remained. Works and words can be restrained, but lust and inclinations no one can root out of himself.

In short, if you desire to attain the true righteousness that avails before God, you must despair altogether of yourself and trust in God alone. You must surrender yourself entirely to Christ and accept Him, so that all He has is yours, and all that is yours becomes His. In this way, you begin to burn with divine love and become quite another person, completely born anew, and all that is in you is converted. Then you will have as much delight in chastity as you had pleasure before in fornication, and so forth with all lusts and inclinations.

This now is the first work of God, that we learn to know ourselves, how condemned, miserable, weak, and sickly we are. It is then God's good will that a man desponds and despairs of himself when he hears, "This shall you do and that shall you do." For everybody must feel and experience in himself that he does not and cannot do it. The Law is neither able nor is it designed to give you this power of obeying it; but it proves what Paul said, *"The Law worketh wrath"* (Romans 4:15), that is, nature rages against the Law and wishes the Law did not exist.

Therefore, those who presume to satisfy the Law by outward deeds become hypocrites, but in the others it only *"worketh wrath"* and causes sins to increase. As Paul said in another place, *"The strength of sin is the law"* (1 Corinthians 15:56). For the Law does not take sin away. It multiplies sin and causes me to feel my sin. So he said again to the Corinthians, *"The letter killeth"* (2 Corinthians 3:6)—that is, the Law works death in you. In other words, it reduces you to nothing, *"but the Spirit giveth life"* (v. 6). For the Law can be fulfilled only when you come to God through the Gospel, as we will hear.

Therefore, the world errs when it tries to make men righteous through laws; only pretenders and hypocrites result from such efforts. But reverse this and say, as Paul said, "The Law produces sin." For the Law does not help me the least, except that it teaches me to know myself; there I find nothing but sin. Then how would it take sin away? We will now see how this thought is set forth in this Gospel. The text says, *"Then the same day at evening, being the first day of the week, when the doors were shut where the disciples were assembled for fear of the Jews…"* (John 20:19).

What did the disciples fear? They feared death; they were in the very midst of death. Where did their fear of death come from? From sin, for if they had not sinned, they would not have feared. Nor could death have injured them; for *"the sting of death,"* which is the means by which it kills, *"is sin"* (1 Corinthians 15:56). But they, like us all, did not yet have a true knowledge of God. For if they had esteemed God as God, they would have been without fear and in security; as David said,

> *Whither shall I go from your spirit? or whither shall I flee from thy presence? If I ascend up into heaven, thou art there: if I make my bed in hell, behold, thou art there. If I take the wings of the morning, and dwell in the uttermost parts of the sea; even there shall thy hand lead me, and thy right hand shall hold me.* (Psalm 139:7–10)

And as he said in another place, *"I will both lay me down in peace, and sleep: for thou, LORD, only makest me dwell in safety"* (Psalm 4:8). It is easy to die, if I believe in God, for then I do not fear death. But whoever does not believe in God must fear death and can never have a joyful and secure conscience.

Now, God drives us to this by holding the Law before us, so that, through the Law, we may come to a knowledge of ourselves. For no one can ever be saved without this knowledge. He who is well needs no physician; but if a man is sick and desires to become well, he must know that he is weak and sick. Otherwise, he cannot be helped. But if one is a fool and refuses to take the remedy that will restore him to health, he will certainly die and perish. But some priests have closed our eyes so that we were not compelled, and not able, to know ourselves. They failed to preach the true power of the Law. For where the Law is not properly preached, there can be no self-knowledge.

David had such knowledge when he said,

*Have mercy upon me, O God, according to thy lovingkindness:
according unto the multitude of thy mercies blot out my transgressions. Wash me thoroughly from mine iniquity, and cleanse me from
my sin. For I acknowledge my transgressions: and my sin is ever
before me. Against thee, thee only, have I sinned, and done this evil
in thy sight: that thou mightest be justified when thou speakest, and
be clear when thou judgest. Behold, I was shapen in iniquity, and in
sin did my mother conceive me.* (Psalm 51:1–5)

In this passage, it is as if David wished to say, "Behold, I am formed
of flesh and blood, which of itself is sin, so that I can do nothing but
sin." For although you restrain your hands and feet or tongue so that
they do not sin, the inclinations and lusts always remain because flesh
and blood are present, no matter where you go, whether to Rome or any
other holy place.

If an upright heart that comes to the point of knowing itself is met
by the Law, it will certainly not seek to help itself by works. Instead, it
confesses its sin and helplessness, its infirmity and sickness, and says,
"Lord God, I am a sinner, a transgressor of Your divine commandments.
Help me, for I am lost." Now, when a man is in such fear and cries out
to God, God cannot refrain from helping him. We see, in this case, that
Christ was not absent long from the disciples tormented by fear but was
soon present, comforting them and saying, "Peace be unto you! Be of
good courage. It is I. Do not fear." The same happens now. When we
come to a knowledge of ourselves through the Law and are now in deep
fear, God awakens us and has the Gospel preached to us, by which He
gives us a joyful and secure conscience.

But what is the Gospel? It is this: God has sent His Son into the
world to save sinners (John 3:16) and to crush hell, overcome death,
take away sin, and satisfy the Law. But what must you do? Nothing but
accept this and look up to your Redeemer and firmly believe that He
has done all this for your good and freely gives it all to you as your own.

In the terrors of death, sin, and hell, you can boldly depend upon it and confidently say, "Although I do not fulfill the Law, although sin is still present and I fear death and hell, nevertheless, from the Gospel I know that Christ has bestowed upon me all His works. I am sure He will not lie. He will surely fulfill His promise. And as a sign of this I have received baptism. For He said to His apostles and disciples, '*Go ye into all the world, and preach the gospel to every creature. He that believeth and is baptized shall be saved; but he that believeth not shall be damned*' (Mark 16:15–16). Upon this I anchor my confidence, for I know that my Lord Christ has overcome death, sin, hell, and the devil, all for my good. For He was innocent, as Peter said, '*Who did no sin, neither was guile found in his mouth*' (1 Peter 2:22). Therefore, sin and death were not able to slay Him, and hell could not hold Him. He has become their Lord and has granted this to all who accept and believe it. All this is effected not by my works or merits, but by pure grace, goodness, and mercy."

Now whoever does not claim this faith for himself must perish, and whoever possesses this faith will be saved. For where Christ is, the Father will come and also the Holy Spirit. There will then be pure grace, no Law; pure mercy, no sin; pure life, no death; pure heaven, no hell. I will comfort myself with the works of Christ, as if I myself had done them. I will no longer concern myself about the outward appearance of holiness, St. James or Rome, rosaries or habits, praying or fasting, priests or monks.

Behold, how beautiful the confidence toward God that arises in us through Christ! You may be rich or poor, sick or well, yet you will always say, "God is mine; I am willing to die, for this is acceptable to my Father, and death cannot harm me. It is swallowed up in victory, as Paul said in 1 Corinthians 15:57. Not through us, but "*thanks be to God*," said he, "*which giveth us the victory through our Lord Jesus Christ*." Therefore, although we must die, we have no fear of death, for its power and might are broken by Christ, our Savior.

So then, you understand that the Gospel is nothing but preaching and glad tidings of how Christ entered into the throes of death for us, took upon Himself all our sins, and abolished them. He did not need to do it, but it was pleasing to the Father. He has bestowed all this upon us, in order that we might boldly stand upon it against sin, death, Satan, and hell. Hence arises great, unspeakable joy, such as the disciples here experienced. The text says, *"Then were the disciples glad, when they saw the Lord"* (John 20:20)—not a Lord who inspired them with terror or burdened them with labor and toil, but a Lord who provided for them and watched over them the way a father is the lord of his estate and cares for his own. Then first they rejoiced most on His account, when He spoke to them, *"'Peace be unto you!'* It is I," and when He had shown them His hands and feet, that is, His works, all of which were to be theirs.

In the same manner, He still comes to us through the Gospel, offers us peace, and bestows His works upon us. If we believe, we have them; if we believe not, we do not have them. For the Lord's hands and feet really signify nothing but His works, which He has done here upon earth for men. And the showing of His side is nothing but the showing of His heart in order that we may see how kind, loving, and fatherlike His mind is toward us. All this is set forth for us in the Gospel as certainly and clearly as it was revealed and shown bodily to the disciples in our text. And it is much better that it is done through the Gospel than if He now entered here by the door, for you would not know Him, even if you saw Him standing before you, even much less than the Jews recognized Him.

The true way to become righteous is not by human commandments but by keeping the commandments of God. Now, nobody can do this except by faith in Christ alone. From this flows love that is the fulfill-ment of the Law, as Paul said in Romans 13:10. And this does not result from the exercise of virtues and good works, as was taught up to this time, which produced only true martyrs of Satan and hypocrites. But faith makes one righteous, holy, chaste, humble, and so forth. For as Paul said to the Romans, "[The Gospel] *is the power of God unto salvation to every one that believeth; to the Jew first, and also to the Greek. For therein is the righteousness of God revealed from faith to faith: as is written, The just shall live by faith*" (Romans 1:16–17). Your works will not save you, but the Gospel will if you believe. Your righteousness is nothing, but Christ's righteousness avails before God. The Gospel speaks of this, and no other writing does. Whoever now wishes to overcome death and blot out sins by his works says that Christ has not died; as Paul said to the Galatians, "*If righteousness come by the law, then Christ is dead in vain*" (Galatians 2:21). And those who preach otherwise are wolves and seducers.

This has been said of the first part of our Gospel, to show what our attitude is to be toward God—namely, we are to cling to Him in faith. It shows what true righteousness is, righteousness that is pleasing to God, and how it is attained—namely, by faith in Christ, who has redeemed us from the Law, death, sin, hell, and the devil, and who has freely given us all this in order that we may rely upon it in defiance of the Law, death, sin, hell, and the devil. Now we will see how we are to conduct ourselves toward our neighbor. This is also shown to us in the text.

OF LOVE TO YOUR NEIGHBOR

The Lord said, "*As my Father hath sent me, even so send I you*" (John 20:21).

Why did God the Father send Christ? For no other purpose than to do the Father's will—namely, to redeem the world. He was not sent to merit heaven by good works or to become righteous. He did many good works; yes, His whole life was nothing else than a continual doing good. But for whom did He do it? For the people who stood in need of it, as we read here and there in the Gospels. All He did, He did for the purpose of serving us. "*As my Father hath sent me,*'" He said here, "'*even so send I you.'* My Father has sent Me to fulfill the Law, take the sin of the world upon Myself, slay death, and overcome hell and the devil—not for My own sake, for I am not in need of it, but all for your sakes and on your behalf, so that I may serve you. So you will do so also."

By faith you will accomplish all this. It will make you righteous before God and save you, and likewise overcome death, sin, hell, and the devil. But you are to show this faith in love, so that all your works may be directed to this end. You are not to seek to merit anything by works, for all in heaven and on earth is yours beforehand. But you are to serve your neighbor by works. For if you do not give forth such proofs of faith, it is certain that your faith is not right. Not that good works are commanded us by this Word. Where faith in the heart is right, there is no need to command good works to be done; they follow by themselves. But the works of love are only an evidence of the existence of faith.

This was also the intent of Peter, when he admonished us in 2 Peter 1:5 to give diligence to make our faith sure and to prove it by our good works. But good works are those we do to our neighbor in serving Him, and the only one thing demanded of a Christian is to love. For by faith he is already righteous and saved. Paul said in Romans 13:8, *"Owe no man any thing, but to love one another: for he that loveth another hath fulfilled the law."* Therefore, Christ said to His disciples in John 13:34–35, *"A new commandment I give unto you, that ye love one another; as I have loved you, that ye also love one another. By this shall all men know that ye are my disciples, if ye have love one to another."*

In this way, we must give proof of ourselves before the world so that everyone may see that we keep God's commandments—yet not as if we would be saved or become righteous by them. So then, I obey the civil government for I know that Christ was obedient to the government, and yet He had no need to be; He did it only for our sakes. Therefore, I will also do it for the sake of Christ, and on behalf of my neighbor, and for the reason alone that I may prove my faith by my love; and so on through all the commandments. In this manner, the apostles exhort us to good works in their writings—not because we become righteous and are saved by them, but only because they prove our faith, both to ourselves and others, and make it sure. The Gospel continues, "*Receive ye the Holy Ghost: whose soever sins ye remit, they are remitted unto them; and whose soever sins you retain, they are retained*" (John 20:22–23).

This power is here given to all Christians, although some have appropriated it to themselves alone, like certain priests have done: They declare publicly and arrogantly that this power was given to them alone and not to the laity. But Christ here spoke neither of priests nor of monks, but said, "*Receive ye the Holy Ghost.*" Whoever has the Holy Spirit, power is given to him—that is, to everyone who is a Christian. But who is a Christian? He who believes. Whoever believes has the Holy Spirit. Therefore, every Christian has the power, as much as priests and monks have in this case, to forgive sins or to retain them.

Do I hear, then, that I can institute confession, baptize, preach, and administer the Lord's Supper? No. Paul said in 1 Corinthians 14:40, "*Let all things be done decently and in order.*" If everybody wished to hear confession, baptize, and administer the Lord's Supper, what order would there be? Likewise, if everybody wished to preach, who would hear? If we all preached at the same time, what a confused babble it would be, like the noise of frogs! Therefore, the following order is to be observed: The congregation will elect one who is qualified, and he will administer the Lord's Supper, preach, hear confession, and baptize. True, we all have this power, but no one will presume to exercise it publicly except the one who has been elected by the congregation to do so. But in private, I may freely exercise it. For instance, if my neighbor comes and says, "Friend, I am burdened in my conscience; speak the absolution to me," then I am free to do so, but I say it must be done privately. If I were to take my seat in the church, and another and all would hear confession, what order and harmony would there be? Let me give an illustration: If there are many heirs among the nobility, they elect one, with the consent of all the others, who alone serves as administrator over the estate on behalf of the others. If everyone wished to rule the country and people, how would it be? Still, they all alike have the power that he who rules has. So it is with this power to forgive sins and to retain them.

But this word, to forgive sins or to retain sins, concerns those who confess and receive more than those who are to impart the absolution. And thereby we serve our neighbor. For in all services the greatest is to release from sin, to deliver from the devil and hell. But how is this done? Through the Gospel, when I preach it to a person and tell him to appropriate the words of Christ and to believe firmly that Christ's righteousness is his own and his sins are Christ's. This, I say, is the greatest service I can render to my neighbor.

The life that one lives only for himself and not for his neighbor is cursed. Conversely, the life that one lives not for himself but for his neighbor—and serves him by teaching, by rebuke, by help, and by whatever manner and means—is blessed. If my neighbor errs, I am to correct him. If he cannot immediately follow me, then I am to bear patiently with him, as Christ did with Judas, who had the purse with the money and transgressed and stole from it. Christ knew this very well; yet He had patience with him, admonished him diligently, although it did no good until he disgraced himself.

So we are to give heed to do everything on behalf of our neighbors and ever to be mindful that Christ has done this and that for me. Why should I not also for His sake freely do all for my neighbor? And see to it that all the works you do are directed not to God, but to your neighbor. Whoever is a ruler, a prince, a mayor, a judge—do not let him think that he is a ruler in order to gain heaven or to seek his own advantage—but to serve the public. And so with other works I assume to do for the good of my neighbor. For example, if I take a wife, I make myself a captive. Why do I do this? So that I may not do harm to my neighbor's wife and daughters, and thus may bring my body into subjection; and so forth with all other works.

Thus we find two thoughts finely portrayed in this Gospel, as in almost all the Gospel lessons—faith and love. Through faith we belong above to God; through love below to our neighbor. May God give us His help so that we may grasp this truth! Amen.

LAW AND GRACE

Charles Spurgeon
Delivered on Sabbath Morning, August 26, 1855,
at New Park Street Chapel, Southwark

*"Moreover the law entered, that the offence might abound. But
where sin abounded, grace did much more abound."*
—Romans 5:20

There is no point upon which men make greater mistakes than upon the relationship that exists between the Law and the Gospel. Some men place the Law above the Gospel; others place the Gospel above the Law. Some modify the Law and the Gospel and preach neither Law nor Gospel, and others entirely nullify the Law by bringing in the Gospel. There are many who think that the Law is the Gospel and teach that men may be saved by good works of benevolence, honesty, righteousness, and sobriety. Such men err. On the other hand, many teach that the Gospel is a Law, that it has certain commands in it, and by obedience to these commands, men earn their salvation. Such men stray from the truth, and do not understand it. A certain class maintain that the Law and the Gospel are mixed, and that men are saved partly by observance of the Law and partly by God's grace. These men do not understand the truth and are false teachers. This morning I will attempt—with God's help—to show you the design of the Law and then the aim of the Gospel. The coming of the Law is explained by its goal: *"Moreover the law entered, that the offence might abound."* Then comes the mission of the Gospel: *"But where sin abounded, grace did much more abound."*

I will consider this text in two senses this morning. First, *as it concerns the world at large and the entrance of the Law into it;* and then afterward, *in regard to the heart of the convinced sinner, and the entrance of the Law into the conscience.*

THE LAW AND GRACE IN THE WORLD

God's purpose in sending the Law into the world was *"that the offence might abound."* But then comes the Gospel, for *"where sin abounded, grace did much more abound."* First, then, in reference to the entire world, God sent the Law into the world *"that the offence might abound."* There was sin in the world long before God sent the Law. God gave His Law so that the offense would appear to be an offense and so the offense might abound exceedingly more than it could have done without the Law's coming. There was sin long before Sinai smoked. Long before the mountain trembled beneath the weight of Deity and the dread trumpet sounded exceedingly loud and long, there had been transgression. And where that Law has never been heard, in heathen countries where that word has never gone forth, yet there is sin—because, though men cannot sin against the Law that they have never seen, yet they can all rebel against the light of nature, against the dictates of conscience, and against that traditional remembrance of right and wrong, which have followed mankind from the place where God created them. All men, in every land, have consciences, and, therefore, all men can sin. The unlearned Hottentot, who has never heard anything of God, has enough of the light of nature that he will discern the difference between the things that are outwardly good or bad. Though he foolishly bows down to stumps and stones, he has judgment, which, if he used it, would teach him better. If he chose to use his talents, he would know there is a God. The apostle, when speaking of men who have only the light of nature, plainly declared that *"the invisible things of him from the creation of the world are clearly seen, being understood by the things that are made, even his eternal power and Godhead; so that they are without excuse"* (Romans 1:20). Without a divine revelation, men can sin, and sin exceedingly— conscience, nature, tradition, and reason are each sufficient to condemn them for their violated commandments.

The Law makes no one a sinner; all men are such since Adam's fall and were so in practice before the Law's introduction. It entered that *"the offence might **abound**."* Now, this seems a very terrible thought at first, and many ministers would have shirked this text altogether. But when I find a verse I do not understand, I usually think it is a text I *should* study; and I try to seek it out before my heavenly Father. Then, when He has opened it to my soul, I consider it my duty to communicate it to you, with the holy aid of the Spirit. *"The law entered, that the offence might abound."* I will attempt to show you how the Law makes offenses *"abound."*

First of all, the Law tells us that *many things are sins that we would never have thought to be so if it had not been for the additional light.*[23] Even with the light of nature, the light of conscience, and the light of tradition, there are some things we would never have believed to be sins if we had not been taught so by the Law. Now, what man, by light of conscience, would keep holy the Sabbath day? Suppose he never read the Bible and never heard of it? If he lived in a South Sea island he might know there was a God, but not by any possibility could he find out that a seventh part of his time should be set apart to that God. We find that there are

---

23. "Let us not dare to dream that God had given us a perfect Law that we poor creatures could not keep, and that therefore He has corrected His legislature and sent His Son to put us under a relaxed discipline. Nothing of the sort. The Lord Jesus Christ has, on the contrary, shown how intimately the Law surrounds and enters into our inward parts in order to convict us of sin within even if we seem clear of it without. Ah me, this Law is high; I cannot attain it. It everywhere surrounds me; it tracks me to my bed and my board; it follows my steps and marks my ways wherever I may be. It does not cease to govern and demand obedience for a moment. O God, I am everywhere condemned, for everywhere Your Law reveals to me my serious deviations from the way of righteousness and shows me how far short I come of Your glory. Have pity on Your servant, for I fly to the Gospel, which has done for me what the Law could never do." *Charles Spurgeon*

certain festivals and feasts among heathens and that they set apart days in honor of their fancied gods; but I would like to know where they could discover that there was a certain *seventh* day to be set apart to God, to spend the time in His house of prayer. How could they, unless tradition may have handed down the fact of the original consecration of that day by the creating Jehovah. I cannot conceive it possible that either conscience or reason could have taught them such a command as this:

> *Remember the sabbath day to keep it holy. Six days shalt thou labor, and do all thy work: but the seventh day is the sabbath of the* LORD *thy God: in it thou shalt not do any work, thou, nor thy son, nor thy daughter, thy manservant, nor thy maidservant, nor thy cattle, nor thy stranger that is within thy gates.* (Exodus 20:8–10)

Moreover, if we include the ceremonial ritual in the term "Law," we can plainly see that many things, which in themselves appear quite harmless, were constituted sins in it. The eating of animals that do not chew their cud and have a divided hoof, wearing of garments made with mixed fabrics, sitting on a bed polluted by a leper—with a thousand other things—all seem to have no sin in them, but the Law made them into sins, and so made offense abound.

A fact that you can verify by looking at the working of your own mind is that *the Law has a tendency to make men rebel.* Human nature rises against restraint. *"I had not known lust except the law had said, Thou shall not covet"* (Romans 7:7). The depravity of man is excited to rebellion by the proclamation of laws. We are so evil that at once we conceive the desire to commit an act, simply because it is forbidden. We all know that children, as a rule, will always desire what they may not have, and if they are forbidden to touch anything, they will either do so at the first opportunity or will long to be able to do so. Any student of human nature can discern the same tendency in humankind at large. Should the Law then be held responsible for my sin? God forbid. *"But sin, taking occasion by the commandment, wrought in me all manner of concupiscence…. For sin, taking occasion by the commandment, deceived me, and by it slew me*" (Romans 7:8, 11). The Law is "*holy, and just, and good*" (v. 12). It is not faulty, but sin uses it as an opportunity for offense and rebels when it ought to obey. Augustine placed the truth in a clear light when he wrote, "The Law is not in fault, but our evil and wicked nature; even as a heap of lime is still and quiet until water is poured on it, but then it begins to smoke and burn, not from the fault of the water, but from the nature of the lime, which will not endure it." Thus, you see, this is a second sense in which the entrance of the Law causes the offense to abound.

Next, the Law *increases the sinfulness of sin by removing all excuse of ignorance.* Until men know the Law, their crimes have at least an excuse of partial ignorance, but when the code of rules is spread before them, their offenses become greater since they are committed against light and knowledge. He who sins against conscience will be condemned; how much sorer a punishment will be due to the one who despises the voice of Jehovah, defies His sacred sovereignty, and willfully tramples on His commands. The more light, the greater the guilt—the Law gives forth that light and so causes us to become double offenders. O you nations of the earth who have heard the Law of Jehovah—your sin is increased, and your offense abounds.

I think I hear some say, "How unwise it must have been that a Law came to make these things abound!" At first sight, does it not seem very harsh that the great Author of the world would give us a Law that will not justify, but instead indirectly cause our condemnation to be greater? Does it not seem to be a thing that a gracious God would not reveal but would instead withhold? But know that "*the foolishness of God is wiser than men*" (1 Corinthians 1:25), and understand that there is a gracious purpose even here. Natural men dream that they will obtain favor by a strict performance of duty, but God says, "I will show them their folly by proclaiming a Law so high that they will despair of attaining it. They think that works will be sufficient to save them. They are wrong, and they will be ruined by their mistake. I will send them a Law so terrible in its judgments, so unflinching it its demands, that they cannot possibly obey it. They will be driven to desperation and will come and accept My mercy through Jesus Christ. They cannot be saved by the Law—not by the Law of nature. As it is, they have sinned against it. I know that, they have foolishly hoped to keep My Law and think that by works of the Law, they may be justified. I have said, *'By the works of the law shall no flesh be justified'* (Galatians 2:16); therefore, I will write a Law—it will be a black and heavy one—a burden that they cannot carry. Then they will turn away and say, 'I will not attempt to perform it; I will ask my Savior to bear it for me.'"

Imagine an example: Some young men are about to go to sea, where I foresee they will meet with a storm. By the time the natural storm comes on, those young men will be a long way out at sea, and they will be wrecked and ruined before they get back to shore and safety. But suppose you put me in a position where I may cause a tempest before the other arises. What do I do? Why, when they are just at the mouth of the river, I send a storm, putting them in the greatest danger and hurling them ashore so that they are saved. This is what God did. He sent a Law that shows humankind the roughness of the journey. The tempest of the Law compels them to return to the harbor of free grace and saves them from a most terrible destruction, which would otherwise overwhelm them.

The Law never came to save men. That never was its intention at all. Its purpose in coming was to make the evidence complete that salvation by works is impossible and, consequently, to drive the elect of God to rely wholly on the finished salvation of the Gospel. Now, just to illustrate my meaning, let me describe it by one more example. You all know of those high mountains called the Alps. Well, it would be a great mercy if those Alps were a little higher. It would have been, in any event, for Napoleon's soldiers when he led his large army over and caused thousands to perish in crossing.

Now, if it would have been possible to pile another Alps onto their summit and make them higher than the Himalayas, would not the increased difficulty have deterred him from his enterprise and so have adverted the destruction of thousands? Napoleon demanded, "Is it possible?" "Barely possible," was the reply. "*Advance*," cried Bonaparte, and the army was soon toiling up the mountainside.

By the light of nature, it *does* seem possible for us to go over this mountain of works, but all men would have perished in the attempt, the path of even its lowest hill being too narrow for mortal footsteps. God, therefore, puts another Law, like a mountain, on the top of the first; and now the sinner says, "I cannot climb over that. It is a task beyond Herculean might. I see before me a narrow pass, called the pass of Jesus Christ's mercy—the pass of the Cross—I think I will make my way there." But if the mountain had not been too high for the sinner, he would have gone climbing up and climbing up, until he sank into some chasm, was lost under some mighty avalanche, or in some other way perished eternally. But the Law came so that the whole world might see the impossibility of being saved by works.

Let us turn to the more pleasing part of the subject—*the superabundance of grace*. Having grieved over the devastations and the hurtful deeds of sin, it delights our hearts to be assured that "*grace did much more abound.*"

Grace excels sin in the numbers it brings beneath its sway. It is my firm belief that the number of the saved will be far greater than the damned. It is written that in all things Jesus will have preeminence (Colossians 1:18). Why is this to be left out? Can we think that Satan will have more followers than Jesus? Oh, no; for while it is written that the redeemed are a multitude that no man can count, it is not recorded that the lost are beyond numeration. True, we know that the visible elect are always a *remnant*, but then there are others to be added.

Think for a moment of the army of infant souls who are now in heaven. These all fell in Adam, but being all elect, they were all redeemed and regenerated and were privileged to fly from their mothers' breasts to glory. Happy lot, which we who are spared might well envy. Nor let it be forgotten that the multitudes of converts in the millennial age will very much turn the scale. For then the world will be exceedingly populous, and a thousand years of a reign of grace might easily suffice to overcome the majority accumulated by sin during six thousand years of its tyranny. In that peaceful period, when all will know Him, from the least even to the greatest, the sons of God will fly like doves to their windows, and the Redeemer's family will be exceedingly multiplied.

Though those who have been deluded by superstition and destroyed by lust must be counted by thousands, grace has still the preeminence. *"Saul hath slain his thousands, and David his ten thousands"* (1 Samuel 18:7). We admit that the number of the damned will be immense, but we also think that the two states of infancy and millennial glory will furnish so great a reserve of saints that Christ will win the day. The procession of the lost may be long; there must be thousands and thousands and thousands of those who have perished, but the greater procession of the King of Kings will be composed of larger hosts than even these. *"Where sin abounded, grace did much more **abound**."* The trophies of free grace will be far more than the trophies of sin.

Yet again. Grace does *"**much** more abound"* because a time will come when the world will be all full of grace—while there has never been a period in this world's history when it was wholly given to sin. When Adam and Eve rebelled against God, there was still a display of grace in the world. In the Garden at the close of the day, God said, *"I will put enmity between thee and the woman, and between thy seed and her seed; it shall bruise thy head, and thou shalt bruise his heel"* (Genesis 3:15). Since that first transgression, there has never been a moment when grace has entirely lost its footing in the earth. God has always had His servants on earth. At times they have been hidden by fifties in the caves, but they have never been utterly cut off. Grace might be low; the stream might be very shallow, but it has never been wholly dry. There has always been a salt of grace in the world to counteract the power of sin. The clouds have never been so thick that they hid the day. But the time is fast approaching when grace will extend over our poor world and be universal.

According to the Bible's testimony, we look for the great day when the dark cloud that has swathed this world in darkness shall be removed, and it will shine once more like all its sister planets. For many long years it has been clouded and veiled by sin and corruption, but the last fire will consume its rags and sackcloth. After that fire, the world will shine in righteousness. The huge molten mass now slumbering in the bowels of our common mother will furnish the means of purity. Palaces, crowns, peoples, and empires are all to be melted down; and after the present creation has been burned up entirely, God will breathe upon the heated mass, and it will cool down again. He will smile on it as He did when He first created it, the rivers will run down the new-made hills, and the oceans will float in new-made channels. The world will be again the abode of the righteous forever and forever. This fallen world will be restored to its orbit; that gem that was lost from the scepter of God will be set again. Yes, He will wear it as a seal around His arm. (See Song of Solomon 8:6.) Christ died for the world, and what He died for He will have. He died for the whole world, and the whole world He will have, when He has purified it and cleansed it and fitted it for Himself. "*Where sin abounded, grace did much more abound*," for grace will be universal, and sin never was.

One thought more: Has the world lost its possessions by sin? It has gained far more by grace. True, we have been expelled from a Garden of delights where peace, love, and happiness found a glorious habitation. True, Eden is not ours, with its luscious fruits, its blissful bowers, and its rivers flowing over sands of gold. But we have through Jesus a fairer habitation. He has *made us sit together in heavenly places* (Ephesians 2:6)—the plains of heaven exceed the fields of Paradise in the ever new delights that they afford, while the Tree of Life and the river from the throne house the inhabitants of the celestial regions in more than a paradise. Did we lose natural life and subject ourselves to painful death by sin? Has grace not revealed an immortality for the sake of which we are too glad to die? Life lost in Adam is more restored in Christ. We admit that our original robes were rent asunder by Adam, but Jesus has clothed us with a divine righteousness, far exceeding in value even the spotless robes of created innocence. We mourn our low and miserable condition through sin, but we will rejoice at the thought that we are now more secure than before we fell, and we are brought into closer alliance with Jesus than our standing could have procured us. O Jesus! You have won us an inheritance more wide than our sin has ever lavished. Your grace has overtopped our sins. "*Grace* [does] *much more abound.*"

THE ENTRANCE OF THE LAW INTO THE HEART

We have to deal carefully when we come to deal with internal things; it is not easy to talk about this little thing, the heart. When we begin to meddle with the Law of their souls, many become indignant, but we do not fear their wrath. We are going to attack the hidden man this morning. The Law entered their hearts that sin might abound, "*but where sin abounded, grace did much more abound.*"

The Law causes the offense to abound by *revealing sin to the soul.* Once the Holy Spirit applies the Law to the conscience, secret sins are dragged to light, little sins are magnified to their true size, and things that appeared harmless become exceedingly sinful.[24] Before that dread searcher of the hearts and trier of the passions makes his entrance into the soul, it appears righteous, just, lovely, and holy; but when he reveals the hidden evils, the scene is changed. Offenses that were once styled slight trifles, fancies of youth, follies, indulgences, or little slips then

---

24. For an illustration of this truth, visit www.livingwaters.com and click on "Are You a Good Person?"

appear in their true colors, as breaches of the Law of God deserving appropriate punishment.

John Bunyan will explain my meaning by an extract from his famous allegory:

> Then the Interpreter took Christian by the hand and led him into a very large parlor that was full of dust because it was never swept. After he had reviewed it a little while, the Interpreter called for a man to sweep. Now, when he began to sweep, the dust began to fly so abundantly about that Christian was almost choked by it. Then said Interpreter to a damsel that stood by, "Bring hither water, and sprinkle the room." When she had done this, the room was swept and cleansed with pleasure. Then said Christian, "What does this mean?"

The Interpreter answered, "This parlor is the heart of a man that was never sanctified by the sweet grace of the Gospel. The dust is his original sin and inward corruption, which have defiled the whole man. He that began to sweep, at first, is the Law. She who brought the water and sprinkled it is the Gospel. Now, whereas you saw that as soon as the first began to sweep, the dust flew about so the room could not be cleansed by him. That you were almost choked therewith is to show thee that the Law, instead of cleansing the heart (by its working) from sin, revives sin (Romans 7:9), puts strength into it (1 Corinthians 15:56), and increases it in the soul (Romans 5:20—even as the Law discovers and forbids sin, for it does not give power to subdue. Again, as you saw the damsel sprinkle the room with water, after which it was cleansed with pleasure, this is to show you that when the Gospel comes in the sweet and precious influences thereof to the heart, then, I say, even as you saw the damsel lay the dust by sprinkling the floor with water, so is sin vanquished and subdued and the soul made clean, through the faith of it, and, consequently, fit for the King of glory to inhabit."

The heart is like a dark cellar, full of lizards, cockroaches, beetles, and all kinds of reptiles and insects, which we do not see in the dark; but the Law opens the shutters and lets in the light, and so we see the evil. Since the Law makes sin apparent, it is written that the Law makes the offense to abound.

Once again, *the Law, when it comes into the heart, shows us how very black we are.* Some of us know that we are sinners. It is very easy to say it. The word *sinner* has only two syllables in it, and there are many who frequently have it on their lips but who do not understand it. They see their sin, but it does not appear exceedingly sinful until the Law comes. We think there is something sinful in our actions, but when the Law comes, we detect their abomination. Has God's holy light ever shone into your souls? Have you had the fountains of your great depravity and evil broken up and been wakened up sufficiently to say, "O God! I have sinned"? Now, if you have your hearts broken up by the Law, you will find the heart is more deceitful than the devil. I can say this of myself. I am very much afraid of my heart; it is so bad. The Bible says, *"The heart is deceitful above all things"* (Jeremiah 17:9). The devil is one of the things; therefore, it is worse than the devil—*"and desperately wicked"* (v. 9). How many do we find who are saying, "Well, I trust I have a very good heart deep down. Things may be a little amiss at the top, but I am very good-hearted at the bottom." If you saw some fruit on the top of a basket that was not quite good, would you buy the basket because they told you, "Yes, but they are good at the bottom"? "No, no," you would say, "they are sure to be best at the top, and if they are bad there, they are sure to be rotten below."

There are many people whose friends would say, "He is good-hearted deep down; he would get drunk sometimes, but he is very good-hearted underneath it all." Never believe it! Men are seldom estimated better than they seem to be. If the outside of the cup or platter is clean, the inside may be dirty, but if the outside is impure, you may always be sure the inside is no better. Most of us put our goods in the window— display all our good things in the front and hide bad things behind. If the Law has entered into our souls, let us, instead of making excuses about ourselves, about the badness of our hearts, bow down and say, "Oh, the sin—oh, the uncleanness—the blackness—the awful nature of our crimes!" "The Law entered that the offense may abound."

The Law reveals the exceeding abundance of sin, *by revealing to us the depravity of our nature*. We are all prepared to charge the serpent with our guilt or to insinuate that we go astray from the force of ill example—but the Holy Spirit dissipates these dreams by bringing the Law into the heart. Then the fountains of the great deep are broken up, the chambers of the imagery are opened, and the innate evil of the very essence of fallen man is discovered.

The Law cuts into the core of the evil; it reveals the seat of the malady and informs us that the leprosy lies deep within. Oh, how the man abhors himself when he sees all his rivers of water turned into blood, and loathsomeness creeping over all his being. He learns that sin is no flesh wound but instead a stab in the heart; he discovers that the poison has impregnated his veins, lies in his very marrow, and has its fountain in his inmost heart. Now he loathes himself and wishes to be healed. Actual sin seems not half so terrible as his sinful nature, and at the thought of what he is, he turns pale and gives up salvation by works as an impossibility.

Having thus removed the mask and shown the desperate case of the sinner, the relentless Law causes the offense to abound yet more by *bringing home the sentence of condemnation*. It mounts the judgment seat, puts on the black cap, and pronounces the sentence of death. With a harsh, unpitying voice, it solemnly thunders forth the words, "Condemned already." It bids the soul prepare its defense, knowing well that all apology has been taken away by its former work of conviction. The sinner is, therefore, speechless, and the Law, with frowning looks, lifts up the veil of hell and gives the man a glimpse of torment. The soul feels that the sentence is just, that the punishment is not too severe, and that it has no right to expect mercy; it stands quivering, trembling, fainting, and intoxicated with dismay until it falls prostrate in utter despair. The sinner puts the rope around his own neck, arrays himself in the attire of the condemned, and throws himself at the foot of the King's throne, with but one thought—"I am vile"—and with one prayer—*"God be merciful to me a sinner"* (Luke 18:13).

Nor does the Law cease its operations even here, for it renders the offense yet more apparent *by revealing the powerlessness occasioned by sin.* It not only condemns, but it also actually kills. He who once thought that he could repent and believe at pleasure finds in himself no power to do either the one or the other.

When Moses smites the sinner, he bruises and mangles him with the first blow; but at a second or a third, the sinner falls down as one dead. I myself have been in such a condition that, if heaven could have been purchased by a single prayer, I would have been damned, for I could no more pray than I could fly. Moreover, when we are in the grave that the Law has dug for us, we feel as if we did not feel, and we grieve because we cannot grieve. The dread mountain lies upon us, making it impossible to stir hand or foot, and when we would cry for help, our voices refuse to obey us. In vain the minister cries, "Repent"; our hard hearts will not melt. In vain he exhorts us to believe. The faith of which he speaks seems to be as much beyond our capacity as the creation of the universe. Ruin is now become ruin indeed. The thundering sentence is in our ears, "Condemned already," another cry follows it, *"Dead in trespasses and sins"* (Ephesians 2:1), and a third, more awful and terrible, mingles its horrible warning, "The wrath to come; the wrath to come." (See Matthew 3:7; Luke 3:7; 1 Thessalonians 1:10.) In the opinion of the sinner, he is now cast out as a corrupt carcass; he expects each moment to be tormented by the worm that never dies and to lift up his eyes in hell. Now is mercy's moment, and we turn the subject from condemning Law to abounding grace.

Listen, O heavy-laden, condemned sinner, while I preach, in my Master's name, super-abounding grace. *Grace excels sin in its measure and capacity.* Though your sins are many, mercy has many pardons. Though they excel the stars, the sands, and the drops of dew in their number, one act of remission can cancel all. Your iniquity, though a mountain, will be cast into the midst of the sea. Your blackness will be washed out by the cleansing flood of your Redeemer's gore. Mark! I said *your* sins, and I meant to say so, for if you are now a Law-condemned sinner, I know you to be a vessel of mercy by that very sign. O hellish sinners, abandoned profligates, outcasts of society, outcasts from the company of sinners themselves—if you acknowledge your iniquity, here is mercy, broad, ample, free, immense, and *infinite*. Remember this, O sinner—

> If all the sins that men have done,
> In will, in word, in thoughts, in deed,
> Since words were made, or time began,
> Were laid on one poor sinner's head,
> The stream of Jesus' precious blood
> Applied, removes the dreadful load.

Yet again, grace excels sin in another thing. *Sin shows us its parent and tells us our heart is the father of it, but grace surpasses sin there and shows the Author of grace—the King of Kings.* The Law traces sin to our heart; grace traces its own origin to God, and

> In His sacred breast I see
> Eternal thoughts of love to me.

O Christian, what a blessed thing grace is, for its source is in the everlasting mountains. Sinner, if you are the vilest in the world, if God forgives you this morning, you will be able to trace your pedigree to

Him, for you will become one of the sons of God and have Him always for your Father. I imagine you as a wretched criminal before the Judge, and I hear Mercy cry, "Discharge him! He is pale, lame, sick, broken—heal him. He is part of a vile race—lo, I will adopt him into my family." Sinner, God takes you for His son! Though you are poor, God says, "I will take you to be Mine forever. You will be My heir. There is your fair Brother. Through a blood tie He is one with you—Jesus is your actual Brother!" Yet how did this change come about? Was it not an act of mercy? *"Grace did much more abound."*

> Grace has put me in the number
> Of the Savior's family.

Grace outdoes sin, for it lifts us higher than the place from which we fell.

And again, *"where sin abounded, grace did much more abound"* because *the sentence of the Law may be reversed, but that of grace never can.* I stand here and feel condemned, but I have a hope that I may be acquitted. There is a dying hope of acquittal still left. But when we are justified, there is no fear of condemnation. I cannot be condemned once I am justified; I am *fully* absolved by grace. I defy Satan to lay hands on me if I am a justified man. The state of justification is an unalterable one and is permanently united to glory.

> *Who shall lay any thing to the charge of God's elect? It is God that justifieth. Who is he that condemneth? It is Christ that died, yea rather, that is risen again, who is even at the right hand of God, who also maketh intercession for us. Who shall separate us from the love of Christ? shall tribulation, or distress, or persecution, or famine, or nakedness, or peril, or sword?...Nay, in all these things we are more than conquerors through him that loved us. For I am persuaded, that neither death, nor life, nor angels, nor principalities, nor powers, nor things present, nor things to come, nor height, nor*

depth, nor any other creature, shall be able to separate us from the love of God, which is in Christ Jesus our Lord.

(Romans 8:33–35, 37–39)

Poor condemned sinner, doesn't this charm you and make you feel your love for free grace? And all this is *yours*. Once your crimes have been blotted out, you will never be charged with them again. The justification of the Gospel is no Arminian sham, which may be reversed if you stray in the future. No, once the debt is paid, it cannot be demanded twice. The punishment, once endured, cannot again be inflicted. Saved, saved, saved, entirely saved by divine grace—you may walk without fear the wide world over.

And yet, once more, just as sin makes us sick and grievous and sad, so grace makes us *far more joyful and free*. Sin causes one to go about with an aching heart until he feels as if the world would swallow him or the mountains hanging above would drop upon him. This is the effect of the Law. The Law makes us sad; the Law makes us miserable. But, poor sinner, grace removes the evil effects of sin upon your spirit. If you do believe in the Lord Jesus Christ, you will go out of this place with a sparkling eye and a light heart. I remember well the morning when I stepped into a little place of worship, as miserable almost as hell could make me, for I was ruined and lost. I had often been at chapels where they spoke of the Law, but I heard not the Gospel. But this day was different. I sat down in the pew as a chained and imprisoned sinner, the Word of God came, and then I went out free. Though I went in miserable as hell, I went out elated and joyful. I sat there black, but I went away whiter than driven snow. God said, *"Though your sins be as scarlet, they shall be as white as snow"* (Isaiah 1:18). Why not accept this as your position, my friend, if you feel yourself a sinner now? All He asks of you is that you feel your need of Him. This you have done, and now the blood of Jesus lies before you. "The Law has entered that sin might abound." If you acknowledge your state and accept His mercy, then you are forgiven; only believe it. Elect, only believe it. It is the truth that you are saved.

Finally, poor sinner, has sin made you unfit for heaven? Grace will make you a fit companion for angels and will make the just, perfect. You who are lost and destroyed by sin today will one day find yourself with a crown upon your head and a golden harp in your hand, exalted to the throne of the Most High. Think, O sinner—if you repent, there is a crown reserved for you in heaven. You who are guiltiest, most lost, and depraved, are you condemned in your conscience by the Law? Then I invite you, in my Master's name, to accept pardon through His blood. He suffered in your stead. He has atoned for your guilt, and you are acquitted. You are an object of His eternal affection. The Law is but a schoolmaster to bring you to Christ. Cast yourself on Him. Fall into the arms of saving grace. No works are required—no fitness, no righteousness, no doings. You are complete in Him who said, *"It is finished"* (John 19:30).

PART TWO:

OPEN-AIR PREACHING

FULFILLING THE CHRISTIAN'S HIGHEST CALLING

"No sort of defense is needed for preaching outdoors, but it would take a very strong argument to prove that a man who has never preached beyond the walls of his meetinghouse has done his duty. A defense is required for services within buildings rather than for worship outside of them." —Charles Spurgeon

"Every great preacher of the Bible was an open-air preacher. Peter was an open-air preacher, Paul was an open-air preacher, and so were Elijah, Moses, and Ezra. More important than all, Jesus Christ Himself was an open-air preacher and preached, for the most part, outdoors. Every great sermon recorded in the Bible was preached in the open air: the sermon on the Day of Pentecost, the Sermon on the Mount, the sermon on Mars Hill, etc." —R. A. Torrey

"I may say that a large proportion of the successes of the Salvation Army have been due, in my human estimation, to our open-air operations.... In the ordinary course of things, we would have, you can easily see, no chance without open-air work." —William Booth

"It is no marvel that the devil does not love field preaching! Neither do I; I love a commodious room, a soft cushion, a handsome pulpit. But where is my zeal if I do not trample all these underfoot in order to save one more soul?"   —John Wesley

"Preach abroad…. It is the cooping yourselves up in rooms that has dampened the work of God, which never was and never will be carried out to any purpose without going into the highways and hedges and compelling men and women to come in."   —John Wesley

"I believe I never was more acceptable to my Master than when I was standing to teach those hearers in the open fields…. I now preach to ten times more people than I would if I had been confined to the churches."   —George Whitefield

"I am well assured that I did far more good to my Lincolnshire parishioners by preaching three days on my father's tomb than I did by preaching three years in his pulpit."   —John Wesley

OPEN-AIR MEETINGS

R. A. Torrey[25]

The following is from Torrey's larger work, "Methods of
Christian Work" (Chapter 6).

THEIR IMPORTANCE AND ADVANTAGES

They are scriptural. Jesus said, "Go out quickly into the streets and lanes
of the city, and bring in hither the poor, and the maimed, and the halt, and
the blind" (Luke 14:21). Every great preacher of the Bible was an open-air
preacher. Peter was an open-air preacher, Paul was an open-air preacher,
and so were Elijah, Moses, and Ezra. More important than all, Jesus
Christ Himself was an open-air preacher and preached, for the most
part, outdoors. Every great sermon recorded in the Bible was preached
in the open air: the sermon on the Day of Pentecost, the Sermon on the
Mount, the sermon on Mars Hill, etc. In this country, we have an idea

25. **R. A. Torrey** (1856–1928) was a Congregational evangelist, teacher, and author, born in
Hoboken, New Jersey. He was educated at Yale University and Yale Divinity School. After a
period of skepticism, he trusted in Jesus Christ as his Savior. Soon after, he pastored in Ohio
and then in Minnesota. In 1889, Dwight L. Moody called Torrey to Chicago to become
superintendent of the school that became known as Moody Bible Institute. He also served as
pastor of the Chicago Avenue Church, now the Moody Memorial Church, for twelve years.

that open-air preaching is for those who cannot get any other place to speak, but across the water they look at it quite differently. Some of the most eminent preachers of Great Britain preach in the open air.

Open-air meetings are portable; you can carry them around. It would be very difficult to carry a church or mission building with you, but there is no difficulty in carrying an open-air meeting with you.[26] You can get an open-air meeting where you could never get a church, mission hall, or even a room. You can have open-air meetings in all parts of the city and all parts of the country.

Open-air meetings are more attractive in the summer than hot, sweltering halls or churches. When on vacation, I used to attend a country church. It was one of the hottest, most stifling, and sleepiest places I have ever entered. It was all but impossible to keep awake while the minister attempted to preach. The church was located in a beautiful grove where it was always cool and shady, but it seemed never to enter the minds of the people to go out of the church into the grove. Of course, only a few people attended the church services. One day, a visiting minister suggested that they have an open-air meeting on the front lawn of a Christian man who had a summer residence nearby. The farmers came to that meeting from miles around, in wagons, on foot, and every other way. There was a splendid crowd in attendance. The country churches would do well in the summer to get out of their church building into some attractive grove nearby.

Open-air meetings will accommodate vast crowds. There are few church buildings, especially in the country, that will accommodate more than one thousand people; but people can be accommodated by the thousands in an open-air meeting. It has been my privilege to speak for several summers in a small country town with less than a thousand

---

26. The essence of evangelism is to *"go ye into all the world"* (Mark 16:15). Modern thought focuses on attracting sinners to a church building rather than going out and getting them. When Jesus said, *"Compel them to come in"* (Luke 14:23), He was referring to the kingdom of God—not a building that many mistakenly call "church." Open-air meetings take the message where it's needed. It takes the light of the Gospel into the darkness of the world.

inhabitants. Of course the largest church building in the town would not accommodate more than five hundred people. The meetings, however, were held in the open air, and people drove to them from forty miles around. At one meeting, we had an attendance of fifteen thousand people. Whitefield was driven to the fields by the action of church authorities, and it was well that he was. Some of his audiences at Moorfields were said to number sixty thousand people.

Open-air meetings are economical. You neither have to pay rent nor hire a janitor. They do not cost anything at all. God Himself furnishes the building and takes care of it. I remember that, at a Christian Workers' Convention, a man was continually complaining that no one would rent a mission hall for him to hold meetings in. At last I suggested to him that he had the entire outdoors, and he could go there and preach until someone rented him a hall. He took the suggestion and was used greatly by God. You do not need to have a cent in your pocket to hold an open-air meeting. The whole outdoors is free.[27]

You can reach men in an open-air meeting that you can reach in no other way. I can tell of instance after instance where men who have not been at church or a mission hall for years have been reached by open-air meetings. The people I have known to be reached and converted through open-air meetings have included thieves, drunkards, gamblers, saloon-keepers, abandoned women,[28] murderers, lawyers, doctors, theatrical people, society people—in fact, pretty much every class.

You can reach backsliders and people who have drifted away from the church. One day, when we were holding a meeting on a street corner in a city, a man in the crowd became interested, and one of our

---

27. What a challenge that is to the motives of those who want a "ministry." There's no cost. You don't need a big building and facilities covering ten acres. Although God can bless you with such a large ministry, you don't need material wealth to reach sinners for the kingdom of God. But though the work is easy to begin, do not expect instant gratification. There's often no applause…not on this side of heaven.

28. This sounds like the early church: "Nor thieves, nor covetous, nor drunkards, nor revilers, nor extortioners, shall inherit the kingdom of God. And such were some of you: but ye are washed, but ye are sanctified, but ye are justified in the name of the Lord Jesus, and by the Spirit of our God" (1 Corinthians 6:10–11).

workers dealt with him. He said, "I am a backslider, and so is my wife, but I have made up my mind to come back to Christ." He was saved and so was his brother-in-law.[29]

Open-air meetings impress people by their earnestness. How often I have heard people say, "There is something in it. See those people talking out there on the street. They do not have any collection, and they come here just because they believe what they are preaching." Remarks like this are made over and over again. Men who are utterly careless about the Gospel and Christianity have been impressed by the earnestness of men and women who go out on to the street to win souls for Christ.

Open-air meetings bring recruits to churches and missions. One of the best ways to fill up an empty church is to send your workers out on the street to hold meetings before the church service is held—or better still, go yourself. When the meeting is over, you can invite people to the church or mission. This is the divinely appointed means for reaching men who cannot be reached in any other way. (See Luke 14:21.) All Christians should hear the words of Christ constantly ringing in their ears: *"Go out quickly into the streets and lanes of the city, and bring in hither the poor."*

Open-air meetings enable you to reach men. One of the great problems of most ministers of the Gospel today is how to reach the men. The average church audience is composed very largely of women and children. One of the easiest ways to reach the men is to go out on the streets, where the men are. Open-air meetings are, as a rule, composed of an overwhelming majority of men.

Open-air meetings are good for the health. An English preacher was told that he would die, that he had consumption. He thought he would make the most of the few months he had allotted to live, so he

---

29. Nowadays there are millions in this category of "backslidden," largely because of the shallow nature of many modern Gospel messages. Many in this group have had false conversions, and will most likely avoid the church at all costs. This is why we must go to them.

went out on the streets and began preaching.[30] The open-air preaching cured his consumption, and he lived for many years. The man then became the founder of a great open-air society.

WHERE TO HOLD OPEN-AIR MEETINGS

To put it simply, in the area that you wish to reach. But a few suggestions may prove helpful.

Where the crowds pass. Find the principal thoroughfare where the crowds gather. You cannot hold your meeting just at that point, as the police will not permit it, but you can hold it just a little to one side of that point. As the crowds pass, they will go to one side and listen to you.

Hold them near crowded tenements. In that way, you can preach to the people in the tenements as well as on the street. They will throw open their windows and listen. Sometimes the audience that you do not see will be as large as the one you do see. You may be preaching to hundreds of people inside the building whom you do not see at all. I knew of a poor sick woman being brought to Christ through the preaching she heard on the street. It was a hot summer night, and her window was open. The preaching came in through the window and so touched her heart that she was won to Christ. It is good to have a good strong voice in open-air preaching, for then you can preach to all the tenements within three or four blocks. Mr. Sankey once sang a hymn that was carried over a mile away and converted a man that far off. I have a friend who occasionally uses a megaphone, which carries his voice to immense distances in his open-air meetings.

Hold meetings near circuses, baseball games, and other places where the people congregate. One of the most interesting meetings I ever held was just outside of a baseball field on Sunday. The game was breaking up inside. We held the meeting outside, just behind the grandstand. As there was no game to see inside, the people listened to the

---

30. Every Christian is in this category. Everyone is terminal and should have the mind-set of this man, for we do not know if today could be our last day on earth.

singing and preaching of the Gospel outside. On another Sunday, we drove down to Sell's circus and had the most motley audience I ever addressed. There were people present from almost every nation under heaven. The circus had advertised a "Congress of Nations," so I had a congress of nations for my open-air meeting, too. On that day, I had a Dutchman, a Frenchman, a Scotsman, an Englishman, an Irishman, and an American preach. We took care at the open-air meeting to invite the people to the evening meeting at the mission. That night, a man came who told us that he was one of the employees of the circus and that he was touched that afternoon by the preaching of the Gospel and had come to learn how to be a follower of the Lord Jesus Christ. He accepted the Savior that night.

Hold meetings in or near parks or other public resorts. Almost every city has its resorts where people go on Sunday. As the people will not go to church, the church ought to go out to the people. Sometimes permission can be secured from the authorities to hold the meetings right in the parks. Wherever this is impossible, they can be held nearby. A man who is now a deacon of our church spent his Sundays at Lincoln Park before he was converted; an open-air meeting was held, and there he heard the Gospel and was converted.

Hold meetings in groves. It would be well if every country church could be persuaded to try this. Get out of the church into a grove somewhere, and you will be surprised at the number of people who will come who would not go near the church at all.

Hold open-air meetings near your missions. If you have a mission, be sure to hold an open-air meeting near it. It is the easiest thing in the world to keep a mission full, even during the summer months, if you hold an open-air meeting in connection with it, but it is almost impossible to do so if you do not.

Hold open-air meetings in front of churches. A good many of our empty churches could be filled if we would only hold open-air meetings in front of them.[31] Years ago, when in London, I went to hear Newman Hall preach. It looked to me like a very orderly and aristocratic church, but when I left the church after the second service, I was surprised to find an open-air meeting in full blast right in front of the church, and people gathered there in crowds from the thoroughfare.

Be careful about the little details in connection with the location. On a hot day, hold the meeting on the shady side of the street; on a cool day, the sunny side. Make it as comfortable for the audience as possible. Never compel the audience to stand with the sun shining in their eyes. Preach with the wind, not against it. Take your own position a little above the part of the audience nearest you—upon a curb, chair, platform, rise in the ground, or anything that will raise your head above others so that your voice will carry.

THINGS TO GET

Get it thoroughly understood between yourself and God that He wants you to do this work and that by His grace you are going to do it, whatever it costs. This is one of the most important things in starting out to do open-air work. You are bound to make a failure unless you settle this at the start. Open-air work has its discouragements, its difficulties, and its almost insurmountable obstacles.[32] Unless you start out knowing that God has called you to the work, and come what will, you will go through with it, you are sure to give it up.

Get permission from the powers that be to hold open-air meetings. Do not get into conflict with the police if you can possibly avoid it. As a rule, it is quite easy to get permission to open-air preach if you go about it in a courteous and intelligent way. Find out what the laws

---

31. You may like to suggest this to your pastor. He may never have thought of it.
32. Often Christians get the wrong impression when they watch our videos of open-air preaching. They don't realize that we have left in the cream and removed plentiful footage of times when we stumbled through the Gospel or preached and hardly drew a crowd. If you open-air preach, there will be failures. You can use them either as stumbling blocks or stepping stones. You can either give up or thank God that you are learning, growing, and trusting Him—no matter what comes your way.

of the city are in this regard, and then observe them. Go to the captain of the precinct, tell him that you wish to hold an open-air meeting, and let him see that you are not a disturber of the peace. Many would-be open-air preachers get into trouble from a simple lack of good sense and common decency.

Get a good place to hold the meeting. Do not start out at random. Study your ground. You should operate like a general. We are told that the Germans studied France as a battleground for years before the Franco-Prussian war broke out; and when the war broke out, there were officers in the German army who knew more about France than the officers in the French army did. Lay your plan of campaign, study your battlefield, pick out the best places to hold the meetings, look over the territory carefully, and study it in all its bearings. There are a good many things to be considered. Do not select what would be a good place for someone to throw a big pan full of dishwater upon you. These little details may appear trivial, but they need to be taken into consideration. It is unpleasant, and somewhat disconcerting, when a man is right in the midst of an interesting exhortation, to have a panful of dishwater thrown down the back of his neck.

Get as large a number of reliable Christian men and women to go with you as possible. Crowds draw crowds. There is great power in numbers. One man can go out on the street alone and hold a meeting; I have done it myself. But if I can get fifteen or twenty reliable people to go with me, I will get them every time. Please note that I have said reliable Christian men and women. Do not take anybody along with you to an open-air meeting that you do not know. Be sure to leave a man who is in the habit of making a fool of himself at home; he may upset your whole meeting. Do not take a man or woman with you who has an unsavory reputation; probably someone in the crowd will know it and shout out the fact. Take only people who are of established reputation and well balanced. Never pick up a stranger out of the crowd and ask him to speak. Someone will come along who appears to be just your sort, but if you ask him to speak, you may wish you had not done so.

Get the best music you can. Get a baby organ and a cornet if you can.[33] Be sure to have good singing if it is possible. If you cannot have good singing, have poor singing, for even poor singing goes a good way in the open air. One of the best open-air meetings I ever attended was where two of us were forced to go out alone. Neither of us was a singer. We started with only one hearer, but a drunken man came along and began to dance to our singing, and a crowd gathered to watch him dance. When the crowd had gathered, I simply put my hand on the drunken man, and said, "Stand still for a few moments." My companion took the drunken man as a text for a temperance sermon, and when he got through, I took him for a text. People began to whisper in the crowd, "I would not be in that man's shoes for anything." The man did us good service that night; He first drew the crowd and then furnished us with a text. The Lord turned the devil's instrument right against him that night. If you can, get a good solo singer. Even a poor solo singer will do splendid work in the open air if he sings in the power of the Spirit. I remember a man who attempted to sing in the open air who was really no singer at all, but God in His wonderful mercy caused the man to sing in the power of the Spirit that night. People began to break down on the street, tears rolled down their cheeks, and one woman was converted right there during the singing of that hymn. Although the hymn was sung miserably from a musical standpoint, the Spirit of God used it for that woman's conversion.

Get the attention of your hearers as soon as possible. When you are preaching in a church, people will often stay even if they are not interested. But unless you get the attention of your audience at once in the open air, one of two things will happen: Either your crowd will leave you or else they will begin to ridicule you. In the first half-dozen sentences, you must get the attention of your hearers. I was once holding

---

33. Of course, today we would use more contemporary instruments, like a guitar.

a meeting in one of the hardest places of a city. There were saloons on three of the four corners and three breweries. The first words I spoke were these: "You will notice the cross on the spire of yonder church," for there were several Catholic churches nearby. By these means, I secured their attention at once, and then I talked to them about the meaning of that cross. On holding a meeting one Labor Day, I started out on the subject of labor. I spoke only a few moments on that subject, then led them around to the subject of the Lord Jesus Christ. Holding a meeting one night in the midst of a hot election, near where an election parade was forming, I started out with the question, "Whom shall we elect?" The people expected a political address, but before long I got them interested in the question of whether or not we should elect the Lord Jesus Christ to be the ruler over our lives.

Get some good tracts.[34] Always have tracts when you hold an open-air meeting. They assist in making permanent impressions and in fixing the truth of the message in the listeners' hearts. Have workers pass through the crowd handing out tracts at the proper time.

Get workers around in the crowd to do personal work. Returning from an open-air meeting years ago in the city of Detroit, I said to a minister who was stopping at the same hotel that we had had several conversions in the meeting. He replied by asking me if a certain man from Cleveland was not in the crowd. I replied that he was. This pastor told me that if I looked into it, I would probably find that the conversions were largely due to that man; while the services were going on, this man had been around in the crowd doing personal work. I investigated and found that it was so.

Get a gospel wagon if you can. Of this we shall have more to say when we speak of Gospel Wagon Work.

---

34. See www.livingwaters.com for tracts to use in your evangelizing.

DON'TS

Don't unnecessarily antagonize your audience. I heard of a man addressing a Roman Catholic audience in the open air and criticizing the Roman Catholic Church[35] and the Pope. That man did not have good sense. Another man attempted a prohibition discourse immediately in front of a saloon. He got a brick instead of votes.

Don't get scared. Let Psalm 27:1 be your motto: *"The LORD is my light and my salvation; whom shall I fear? the LORD is the strength of my life; of whom shall I be afraid?"*[36] There is no need to be scared. You may be surrounded by a crowd of yelling hoodlums, but you may be absolutely certain that you will not be hurt unless the Lord wants you to be hurt; and if the Lord wants you to be hurt, that is the best thing for you. You may be killed if the Lord sees fit to allow you to be killed, but it is a wonderful privilege to be killed for the Lord Jesus Christ. One night I was holding a meeting in one of the worst parts of Chicago. Something happened to enrage a part of the crowd that gathered around me. Friends near at hand were in fear lest I be killed, but I kept on speaking and was not even struck.

Don't lose your temper. Whatever happens, never lose your temper. You should never get angry under any circumstances, but it is especially foolish to do so when you are holding an open-air meeting. You will doubtless have many temptations to lose your temper, but never do it. It is very hard to hit a man when he is serene, and if you preserve your serenity, the chances are that you will escape unscathed. Even if a tough strikes you, he cannot do so a second time if you remain calm. Serenity is one of the best safeguards.

---

35. This doesn't mean that you don't expose error in the Roman Catholic Church. However, there are ways to do this without closing the minds of your hearers. For instance, you can say, "It doesn't matter whether you are Roman Catholic or Protestant; if you are not born again, the Bible says that you will not enter the kingdom of God." We must remember that there are often errors in some Protestant churches as well.
36. See longer note at the end of this section.

Don't let your meeting be broken up. No matter what happens, hold your ground if you can, and you generally can. One night I was holding a meeting in a square in one of the most desperate parts of a large city. The steps of an adjacent saloon were crowded with men, many of whom were half drunk. A man came along on a load of hay, went into the saloon, and fired himself up with strong drink. Then he attempted to drive right down upon the crowd in the middle of the square, in which there were many women and children. Some man stopped his horses, and the infuriated man came down from the load of hay, and the howling mob swept down from the steps of the saloon. Somehow or other, the drunken driver got a rough handling in the mob, but not one of our number was struck. Two policemen in citizens' clothes happened to be passing by and stopped the riot. I said a few words more and then formed our little party into a procession, behind which the crowd fell in, and marched down to the mission singing.

Don't fight. Never fight under any circumstances. Even if they almost pound the life out of you, refuse to fight back.[37]

Don't be dull. Dullness will kill an open-air meeting at once. Prissiness will drive the whole audience away. In order to avoid being dull, do not preach long sermons. Use a great many striking illustrations. Keep wide awake yourself, and you will keep the audience awake. Be energetic in your manner. Talk so people can hear you. Don't preach, but simply talk to people.

Don't be soft. The crowd cannot and will not stand one of these nice, namby-pamby, sentimental sort of fellows in an open-air meeting. The temptation to throw a brick or a rotten apple at him is perfectly irresistible, and one can hardly blame the crowd.

Don't read a sermon. Whatever may be said in defense of reading essays in the pulpit, it will never do in the open air. It is possible to have no notes at all. If you cannot talk long without notes, so much the

---

37. See longer note at the end of this section.

better; you can talk as long as you ought to. If you read, you will talk longer than you ought to.

Don't use "cant" or jargon. Use language that people are acquainted with, but do not use vulgar language. Some people think it is necessary to use slang, but slang is never admissible. There is language that is popular and easily understood by the people that is purest Anglo-Saxon.

Don't talk too long. You may have a number of talks in an open-air meeting, but do not have any of them over ten or fifteen minutes long. As a rule, do not have them as long as that. Of course there are exceptions to this, such as when a great crowd is gathered to hear some person in the open air. Under such circumstances, I have heard a sermon an hour long that held the interest of the people. But this is not true in the ordinary open-air meeting.

THINGS ABSOLUTELY NECESSARY TO SUCCESS

Consecrated men and women. None but consecrated men and women will ever succeed in open-air meetings.[38] If you cannot get such, you might as well give up holding open-air meetings.

Dependence on God. There is nothing that will teach someone his dependence on God more quickly and more thoroughly than holding open-air meetings. You never know what is going to happen. You cannot lay plans that you can always follow in an open-air meeting. You never know what moment someone will come along and ask some troublesome question. You do not know what unforeseen event is going to occur. All you can do is depend on God—but that is perfectly sufficient.[39]

Loyalty to the Word of God. It is the man who is absolutely loyal to God's Word, and who is familiar with it and constantly uses it, who succeeds in the open air. God often takes a text that is quoted and uses

---

38. See longer note at the end of this section.
39. See longer note at the end of this section.

it for the salvation of some hearer. Arguments and illustrations are forgotten, but the text sticks and converts.

Frequently filling anew with the Holy Spirit. If any man needs to take advantage of the privilege of fresh infillings of the Holy Spirit, it is the open-air worker. Spiritual power is the great secret of success in this,[40] as in all other Christian work.

---

40. See longer note at the end of this section.

NOTES

36. You may have a few concerns. Perhaps one of them is the thought of someone verbally disagreeing with what you say. These folks are what are known as "hecklers." The best thing that can happen to an open-air meeting is to have a good heckler. Jesus gave us some of the greatest gems of Scripture because some heckler either made a statement or asked a question in an open-air setting.

A good heckler can increase a crowd of twenty people to two hundred in a matter of minutes. The air becomes electric. Suddenly, you have two hundred people listening intently to how you will answer a heckler. All you have to do is remember the attributes of 2 Timothy 2:23–26: Be patient, gentle, humble. Don't worry if you can't answer a question. Just say, "I can't answer that, but I'll try to get the answer for you if you really want to know." With Bible "difficulties," I regularly fall back on this powerful statement from Mark Twain: "Most people are bothered by those passages of Scripture they don't understand, but for me I have always noticed that the passages that bother me are those I do understand."

A "good" heckler is one who will provoke your thoughts. He will stand up, speak up, and then shut up so that you can preach. Occasionally, you will get hecklers who have the first two qualifications, but they just won't be quiet. If they will not let you get a word in, move your location. Most of the crowd will follow. It is better to have ten listeners who can hear than two hundred who can't. If the heckler follows, move again. At this point, the crowd will usually turn on him. One ploy that often works with a heckler who is out solely to hinder the Gospel is to wait until he is quiet and then say to the crowd (making sure that the heckler is listening as well), "I want to show you how people are like sheep. When I move, watch this man follow me because he can't get a crowd by himself." His pride will usually keep him from following.

If you have a "mumbling heckler," one who won't speak up, ignore him and talk over top of him. This will usually get him angry enough to speak up and draw hearers. Be careful, though; there is a fine line between him getting angry enough to draw a crowd and him hitting you. Don't worry; you will find it in time. If you are fortunate enough to get a heckler, don't panic. Show him genuine respect—not only because he can double your crowd, but also because the Bible says to honor all men. Ask the heckler his name so that if you want to ask him a question and he is talking to someone, you don't have to say, "Hey, you!"

Often, people will walk through the crowd so they can get close to you and will whisper something like, "I think you are a #@*!$!" Answer loud enough for the crowd to hear, "God bless you." Do it with a smile so that it looks as though the person has just whispered a word of encouragement to you. This will stop him from doing it again. The Bible says to bless those who curse you, and to do good to those who hate you. Remember that you are not fighting against flesh and blood. Hecklers will stoop very low; they will be cutting and cruel in their remarks. If you have some physical disability, they will play on it. Try to smile back at them. Look past the words. If you are reviled for the name of Jesus, *"rejoice, and be exceeding glad"* (Matthew 5:12). Read Matthew 5:10–12 until it is written on the corridors of your mind. The most angry hecklers are usually what we call "backsliders." These are actually false converts who never slid forward in the first place. They "asked Jesus into their heart" but never truly repented. Ask such a heckler, "Did you know the Lord?" (See Hebrews 8:11.) If he answers yes, then he is admitting that he willfully denies the Lord. If he answers no, then he was never a Christian in the first place—*"This is eternal life, that they might know You, the only true God, and Jesus Christ, whom You have sent"* (John 17:3 NKJV).

37. When you're preaching open-air, don't let angry reactions from the crowd concern you.

A dentist knows where to work on a patient when he touches a raw nerve. When you touch a raw nerve in the heart of the sinner, it means that you are in business. Anger is a thousand times better than apathy. Anger is a sign of conviction. If I have an argument with my wife and suddenly realize that I am in the wrong, I can come to her in a repentant attitude and apologize, or I can attempt to save face by lashing out in anger. Angry responses indicate that you are affecting your audience.

Read Acts 19 and see how Paul was a dentist with an eye for decay. He probed raw nerves wherever he went. At one point, he had to be carried at shoulder height by soldiers because of the *"violence of the people"* (Acts 21:35). Now that is a successful preacher! He didn't seek the praise of men. John Wesley told his evangelist trainees that when they preached, people should either get angry or get converted. No doubt, he wasn't speaking about the "Jesus loves you" Gospel, but about sin, Law, righteousness, judgment, and hell.

38. Whenever you are in an open-air situation, be suspicious of so-called Christians who are intent on distracting workers from witnessing. They argue about prophecy, or how much water one should baptize with, or in whose name they should be baptized. It is grievous to see five or six Christians standing around arguing with some sectarian nitpicker while sinners are sinking into hell.

There is one passage in Scripture to which I point for all those who want to witness or preach in the open air. It is 2 Timothy 2:24–26. Memorize it. Scripture tells us that sinners are blind. They cannot see. What would you think if I were to stomp up to a blind man who had just stumbled, and say, "Watch where you're going, blind man!"? Such an attitude is completely unreasonable. The man cannot see. The same applies to the lost—spiritual sight is beyond their ability. Look at the words used in Scripture: *"Except a man be born again, he cannot see the kingdom of God"* (John 3:3). *"The god of this world hath blinded the minds of them which believe not"* (2 Corinthians 4:4). *"But the natural man receiveth not the things of the Spirit of God: for they are foolishness to him: neither can he know them"* (1 Corinthians 2:14). *"Having the understanding darkened...because of the blindness of their heart"* (Ephesians 4:18). *"Ever learning, and never able to come to the knowledge of the truth"* (2 Timothy 3:7). With these thoughts in mind, read 2 Timothy 2:24–26 again and look at the adjectives used by Paul to describe the attitude we are to have with sinners: *"must not strive...be gentle...patient...in meekness."* Just as it is unreasonable to be impatient with a blind man, so it is with the sinner.

The Bible warns us to avoid foolish questions because they start arguments (2 Timothy 2:23). Most of us have fallen into the trap of jumping at every objection to the Gospel. However, these questions can often be arguments in disguise to sidetrack you from the *"weightier matters of the law"* (Matthew 23:23). While apologetics (arguments for God's existence, creation vs. evolution, etc.) are legitimate in evangelism, they should be merely "bait," with the Law of God being the "hook" that brings the conviction of sin. Those who witness solely in the realm of apologetical argument may get only an intellectual decision instead of a repentant conversion. The sinner may come to a point of acknowledging the Bible as the Word of God and Jesus as Lord—but even the devil knows that. (See James 2:19.) Always pull the sinner back to his responsibility before God on Judgment Day, as Jesus did in Luke 13:1–5.

39. As you share the Gospel, divorce yourself from the thought that you are merely seeking "decisions for Christ." What we should be seeking is repentance within the heart. This is the purpose of the Law, to bring the knowledge of sin. How can a man repent if he doesn't know what sin is? If there is no repentance, there is no salvation. Jesus said, *"Unless you repent you will all likewise perish"* (Luke 13:3 NKJV). God is *"not willing that any should perish, but that all*

should come to repentance" (2 Peter 3:9).

Many don't understand that the salvation of a soul is not a resolution to change a way of life, but *"repentance toward God, and faith toward our Lord Jesus Christ"* (Acts 20:21). The modern concept of success in evangelism is measured by how many people were "saved" (that is, how many prayed "the sinner's prayer"). This produces a "no decisions, no success" mentality. This shouldn't be, because Christians who seek decisions in evangelism become discouraged after a time of witnessing if "no one came to the Lord." The Bible tells us that as we sow the good seed of the Gospel, one sows and another reaps. If you faithfully sow the seed, someone will reap. If you reap, it is because someone has sown in the past. It is always God who causes the seed to grow. If His hand is not on the person you are leading in a prayer of committment, if there is not God-given repentance, then you will end up with a stillbirth on your hands, and that is nothing to rejoice about. We should measure our success by how faithfully we sowed the seed. In that way, we will avoid becoming discouraged.

40. It is obvious from Scripture that God requires us not only to preach to sinners, but also to teach them. The servant of the Lord must be *"apt to teach, patient, in meekness instructing"* those who oppose him (2 Timothy 2:24–25). For a long while, I thought I was to leap among sinners, scatter the seed, then leave. But our responsibility goes further. We are to bring the sinner to a point of understanding his need before God. Psalm 25:8 says, *"Good and upright is the LORD: therefore will he teach sinners in the way."* Psalm 51:13 affirms, *"Then will I teach transgressors thy ways; and sinners shall be converted unto thee."* The Great Commission is to teach sinners: *"Teach all nations...teaching them to observe all things"* (Matthew 28:19–20). The disciples obeyed the command: *"Daily in the temple, and in every house, they ceased not to **teach** and preach Jesus Christ"* (Acts 5:42, emphasis added). The "good-soil" hearer is he who *"heareth...and understandeth"* (Matthew 13:23).

Philip the evangelist saw fit to ask his potential convert, the Ethiopian, *"Do you understand what you are reading?"* (Acts 8:30 NKJV). Some preachers are like a loud gun that misses the target. It may sound effective, but if the bullet misses the target, the exercise is in vain. He may be the largest-lunged, chandelier-swinging, pulpit-pounding preacher this side of the book of Acts. He may have great teaching on faith, and everyone he touches may fall over, but if the sinner leaves the meeting failing to understand his desperate need of God's forgiveness, then the preacher has failed. He has missed the target, which is the understanding of the sinner. This is why the Law of God must be used in preaching. It is a *"schoolmaster"* (Galatians 3:24–25) to bring *"the knowledge of sin"* (Romans 3:20). It teaches and instructs. A sinner will come to "know His will, and approve the things that are most excellent" (see Acts 22:14; Philippians 1:10), if he is *"instructed out of the Law"* (Romans 2:18).

One of the most difficult things to do is draw a crowd to hear the Gospel. Today's society has been programmed to want immediate action, and open-air preaching isn't too attractive to guilty sinners. Therefore, we have to be as wise as serpents and as gentle as doves. (See Matthew 10:16.) A serpent gets its heart's desire subtly.

OPEN-AIR PREACHING

John Wesley[41]

In London, the better; if it becomes a nuisance to some, it will be a blessing to others—if properly conducted. If the Gospel is spoken, and if the spirit of the preacher is one of love and truth, the results cannot be doubted: The bread cast upon the waters must be found after many days. (See Ecclesiastes 11:1.) At the same time, it must be the Gospel, and it must be preached in a manner worth the hearing, for mere noise-making is an evil rather than a benefit.

---

41. On February 17, 1739, the fire of the First Great Awakening was sparked. George Whitefield said, "I have now taken the field. Some may censure me, but is there not a cause? Pulpits are denied, and the poor coal miners are ready to perish for lack of knowledge." Whitefield needed help with his ministry, so he called on his beloved friend, John Wesley. Wesley observed Whitefield open-air preaching and said, "I can hardly reconcile myself at first to this strange way of preaching in the fields...having been all my life, till very lately, so tenacious of every point relating to decency and order, that I should have thought the saving of souls almost a sin if it had not been done in a church." However, he became convinced that this was not only biblical, but also the most effective way to reach the lost. John Wesley preached about fifteen sermons a week for fifty-three years. He preached over forty thousand sermons and traveled on horseback two hundred twenty thousand miles to open-air preach. If you can find a copy of John Wesley's Journal, it is worth reading. He makes the most zealous of us seem lukewarm.

I know a family almost driven out of their senses by the hideous shouting of monotonous exhortations[42] and the howling of "Safe in the arms of Jesus" near their door every Sabbath afternoon for an entire year. I once saw a man preaching with no hearer but a dog, who sat upon his tail and looked up very reverently while his master orated. There were no people at the windows or passing by, but the brother and his dog were at their post whether the people would hear or whether they would forbear. Once also I passed an earnest orator whose hat was on the ground before him, filled with papers, and there was not even a dog for an audience, nor anyone within hearing; yet he did "waste his sweetness on the desert air." I hope it relieved his own mind. Really it must be viewed as an essential part of a sermon that somebody should hear it: It cannot be a great benefit to the world to have sermons preached in a vacuum.

As to style in preaching outdoors, it should certainly be very different from much of what prevails within, and perhaps if a speaker were to acquire a style fully adapted to a street audience, he would be wise to bring it indoors with him. A great deal of sermonizing may be defined as saying nothing at extreme length; but outdoors verbosity is not admired. You must say something and have done with it and go on to say something more, or your hearers will let you know.

"Now then," cries a street critic, "let us have it, old fellow." Or maybe the observation is made, "Now then, pitch it out! You'd better go home and learn your lesson." "Cut it short, old boy," is a very common admonition,[43] and I wish the presenters of this free advice could let it be heard inside Bethel and Zoar[44] and some other places sacred to long-winded orations. Where these outspoken criticisms are not employed, the

---

42. These folks are still around today, and they still do damage to the cause of Christ. It seems that they lack common sense, the ability to reason, and any knowledge that it is the *Gospel* that is the power of God unto salvation, and that it is the Gospel that they should be preaching.
43. Today's hecklers are not so polite, and their language is a little more colorful.
44. Bethel and Zoar were two of the "megachurches" of Wesley's day.

hearers rebuke wordiness by quietly walking away.[45] It is very unpleasant to find your congregation dispersing, but it is also a very plain suggestion that your ideas are also much dispersed.

In the street, a man must keep himself lively, use many illustrations and anecdotes, and sprinkle a quaint remark here and there. To dwell long on a point will never do. Reasoning must be brief, clear, and soon done with. The discourse must not be labored or involved, neither must the second point depend upon the first, for the audience is a changing one, and each point must be complete in itself. The chain of thought must be taken to pieces and each link melted down and turned into bullets: You will not need Saladin's saber to cut through a muslin handkerchief as much as Coeur de Lion's battle-ax to break a bar of iron. Come to the point at once, and come there with all your might.[46]

Short sentences of words and short passages of thought are needed for the outdoors. Long paragraphs and long arguments had better be reserved for other occasions. In quiet country crowds, there is much force in an eloquent silence, now and then interjected; it gives people time to breathe and to reflect. Do not, however, attempt this in a London street; you must go ahead, or someone else may run off with your congregation. In a regular field sermon, pauses are very effective and are useful in several ways, both to speaker and listeners, but to a passing company that is not inclined for anything like worship, a quick, short, sharp address is most appropriate.

In the streets, a man must be intense from beginning to end and, for that very reason, he must be condensed and concentrated in his thought and utterance. It would never do to begin by saying, "My text, dear friends, is a passage from the inspired Word, containing doctrines of the utmost importance and bringing before us in the clearest manner the

---

45. To view open-air preaching in action, complete with hecklers, see "Open-Air Preaching" on video and DVD at www.livingwaters.com.

46. In other words, speak with *passion*. We are *pleading* with men and women who may never hear the Gospel again and may be snatched into death and hell in a moment. We must be both passionate and to the point.

most valuable practical instruction. I invite your careful attention and the exercise of your most candid judgment while we consider it under various aspects and place it in different lights, in order that we may be able to perceive its position in the analogy of the faith. In its exegesis we shall find an arena for the cultured intellect and the refined sensibilities. As the swirling brook meanders among the meadows and fertilizes the pastures, so a stream of sacred truth flows through the remarkable words that now lie before us. It will be well for us to divert the crystal current to the reservoir of our meditation, that we may quaff the cup of wisdom with the lips of satisfaction."

There, friends, is not that rather above the average of word-spinning, and is not that art very generally in vogue in these days? If you go out to the obelisk in Blackfriars Road and talk in that fashion, you will be saluted with "Go on, old buffer," or "Ain't he fine? My eye!" A very vulgar youth might cry, "What a mouth for a tater!" and another will shout in a tone of mock solemnity, "Amen!" If you give them chaff, they will cheerfully return it into your own bosom. Good measure, pressed down and running over, will they mete out to you. (See Luke 6:38.) Shams and shows will have no mercy from a street gathering.

But have something to say, look them in the face, say what you mean, put it plainly, boldly, earnestly, courteously, and they will hear you. Never speak against time or for the sake of hearing your own voice, or you will obtain some information about your personal appearance or manner of oratory that will probably be more true than pleasing. "Crikey," says one, "wouldn't he do for an undertaker! He'd make 'em weep." This was a compliment paid to a melancholy brother whose tone is especially funereal. "There, old fellow," said a critic on another occasion, "you go and wet your whistle. You must feel awfully dry after jawing away at that rate about nothing at all." This also was specially appropriate to a very solemn brother of whom we had often remarked that he would make a good martyr, for there was no doubt of his burning well, he was so dry.

It is sad, very sad, that such rude remarks would be made, but there is a wicked vein in some of us that makes us take note that the vulgar observations are often very true,[47] and "hold as 'twere the mirror up to nature." As a caricature often gives you a more vivid idea of a man than a photograph would afford you, so these rough mob critics strike an orator to life by their exaggerated censures. The very best speaker must be prepared to take his share of street wit, and to return it if need be;[48] but primness, demureness, formality, sanctimonious long-windedness, and the affectation of superiority actually invite offensive pleasantries— and to a considerable extent deserve them. The less you are like a parson, the more likely you are to be heard; and if you are known to be a minister, the more you show yourself to be a man, the better. "What do you get for that, governor?" is sure to be asked if you appear to be a cleric; it will be well to tell them at once that this is extra, that you are doing overtime, and that there is to be no collection. "You'd do more good if you gave us some bread or a drop of beer instead of those tracts," is constantly remarked; but a manly manner and the outspoken declaration that you seek no wages but their good will silence that stale objection.[49]

The *action* of the street preacher should be of the very best. It should be purely natural and unconstrained. No speaker should stand up in the street in a grotesque manner, or he will weaken himself and invite attack. The street preacher should not imitate his own minister, or the crowd will spy out the imitation very speedily if the brother is anywhere near home. Neither should he strike an attitude as little boys do who

---

47. Sometimes it does pay to take notice of our critics, even if they are cruel. If someone hollers, "That doesn't make any sense!" then apologize to him for that fact and start again. Go through the Law, and then explain sin, judgment, the Cross, repentance, and faith. Then sincerely ask, "Does that make sense now?" They will usually admit that it does, for fear you will start over again.

48. Make sure it is street wit rather than sarcasm or the type of humor that humiliates. A laugh from the crowd can be regretted when a few minutes later a sincere person openly accuses you of humiliating someone. No matter how nasty your heckler, you will find it difficult to justify yourself in light of the scriptural admonition for us to be "blameless."

49. It is always good to remind your hearers of your motives. You don't want their money. You are not telling them to join a church. You are there because you care about them and their eternal welfare.

say, "My name is Norval." The stiff straight posture with the regular up-and-down motion of arm and hand is too commonly adopted, but it is not worthy of imitation. And I would even more condemn the wild raving maniac posture that some are so fond of,[50] which seems to be a cross between Whitefield with both his arms in the air and Saint George with both his feet violently engaged in trampling on the dragon. Some good men are grotesque by nature, and others take great pains to make themselves so. Clumsy, heavy, jerky, and cranky legs and arms appear to be liberally dispensed. Many speakers don't know what upon earth to do with these limbs, and so they stick them out, or make them revolve in the queerest manner. The wicked Londoners say, "What a cure!" I only wish I knew of a cure for the evil.

All mannerisms should be avoided. Just now I observe that nothing can be done without a very large Bagster's Bible[51] with a limp cover. There seems to be some special charm about the large size, though it almost needs a little baby buggy in which to push it about. With such a Bible, full of ribbons, select a standing near Seven Dials,[52] after the pattern of a divine so graphically described by Mr. McCree. Take off your hat, put your Bible in it, and place it on the ground. Let the kind friend who approaches you on the right hold your umbrella. See how eager the dear man is to do so! Is it not pleasing? He assures you he is never as happy as when he is helping good men to preach to the poor sinners in these wicked places. Now close your eyes in prayer. When your devotions are over, *somebody will have profited by the occasion.* Where is your affectionate friend who held your umbrella and your hymnbook? Where is that well-brushed hat and that orthodox Bagster? Where? Oh, where? Echo answers, "Where?"

---

50. I have seen an open-air preacher throwing his arms about, sometimes squatting, and then swinging himself around in such a melodramatic fashion, he was nothing short of an embarrassment.

51. Bagster's Bible was a popular reference handbook in Wesley's day. It provided definitions of biblical terms, comparison of Scripture translations, a list of Christ's names, and other useful information for the Bible scholar.

52. Seven Dials: a famous column in London with seven sun dials.

The catastrophe that I have thus described suggests that a brother had better attend you in your earlier ministries, that one may watch while the other prays. If a number of friends will go with you and make a ring around you it will be a great acquisition; and if these can sing it will be still further helpful. The friendly company will attract others, will help to secure order, and will do good service by sounding forth sermons in song.

It will be very desirable to speak so as to be heard, but there is no use in incessant yelling. The best street preaching is not what is done at the top of your voice, for it is impossible to lay the proper emphasis upon key passages when you are shouting with all your might the entire time.[53] When there are no hearers near you but people standing on the other side of the road to listen, would it not be well to cross over and so save a little of the strength that is now wasted?

A quiet, penetrating, conversational style would seem to be the most effective. Men do not bawl and holler when they are pleading in deepest earnestness; they have generally at such times less wind and a little more rain, less rant and a few more tears. On, on, on with one monotonous shout and you will weary everybody and wear out yourself. Therefore, be wise now, you who would succeed in declaring your Master's message among the multitude, and use your voices as common sense would dictate.

---

53. Find your own volume level so that you are speaking loud enough to be heard but not too loud so as to be offensive or to strain your voice. If you don't eat before you preach (with no amplification), you should end up with strained stomach muscles, a good sign that you are using your diaphragm to project your voice rather than your throat. If you solely use your throat, your voice may not last very long and you may do damage to your voice.

OPEN-AIR PREACHING: A SKETCH OF ITS HISTORY AND REMARKS THEREON

Charles Spurgeon

Some customs cannot be defended except by saying that they are very old. In such cases antiquity is of no more value than the rust upon a counterfeit coin. It is, however, a happy circumstance when the usage of ages can be pleaded for a really good and scriptural practice, for it infuses it with a halo of reverence. Now, it can be argued, with little fear of refutation, that open-air preaching is as old as preaching itself. We are at full liberty to believe that when Enoch, the seventh from Adam, prophesied, he asked for no better pulpit than the hillside, and that Noah, as a preacher of righteousness, was willing to reason with his contemporaries in the shipyard in which his marvelous ark was built.

Certainly Moses and Joshua found their most convenient place for addressing vast assemblies beneath the unpillared arch of heaven. Samuel closed a sermon in the field of Gilgal amid thunder and rain, by which the Lord rebuked the people and drove them to their knees. Elijah stood on Carmel and challenged the vacillating nation with, *"How long halt ye between two opinions?"* (1 Kings 18:21).

Jonah, whose spirit was somewhat similar, lifted up his cry of warning in the streets of Nineveh, and in all her gathering places gave forth the warning utterance, *"Yet forty days, and Nineveh shall be overthrown"* (Jonah 3:4). To hear Ezra and Nehemiah, *"all the people gathered themselves together as one man into the street that was before the water gate"* (Nehemiah 8:1). Indeed, we find examples of open-air preaching everywhere in the records of the Old Testament.

It may satisfy us, however, to go back as far as the origin of our own holy faith, and there we hear the forerunner of the Savior crying in the wilderness and lifting up his voice from the river's bank. Our Lord Himself, who is even more our pattern, delivered the larger portion of His sermons on the mountain's side, or by the seashore, or in the streets. Our Lord was, for all intents and purposes, an open-air preacher.[54] He did not remain silent in the synagogue, but He was equally at home in the field. We have no record of His discourse in the royal chapel, but we have the Sermon on the Mount and the Sermon in the Plain—so the very earliest and most divine kind of preaching was practiced outdoors by Him who spoke as never any other man spoke.

There were gatherings of His disciples within walls after His decease, especially the one in the Upper Room; but the preaching even then was most frequently in the court of the temple or in such other open spaces as were available. The notion of holy places and consecrated meetinghouses had not occurred to them as Christians; they preached in the temple, or in such other open spaces as were available, but with equal earnestness *"in every house, they ceased not to teach and preach Jesus Christ"* (Acts 5:42).

It would be very easy to prove that revivals of religion have usually been accompanied, if not caused, by a considerable amount of outdoor

54. We need no further admonition; Jesus of Nazareth was an open-air preacher, and we are called to imitate Him.

preaching or preaching in unusual places. The first avowed preaching of Protestant doctrine was almost necessarily in the open air, or in buildings that were not dedicated to worship, for these were in the hands of the Catholic Church. True, Wycliffe for awhile preached the Gospel in the church at Lutterworth, and Huss, Jerome, and Savonarola for a time delivered semi-Gospel addresses in connection with the ecclesiastical arrangements around them; but when they began more fully to know and proclaim the Gospel, they were driven to find other platforms.

The Reformation, when yet a babe, was like the newborn Christ, and had *"not where to lay* [its] *head"* (Matthew 8:20; Luke 9:58); but a company of men comparable to the heavenly host proclaimed it under the open heavens, where shepherds and common people heard them gladly. Throughout England, we have several trees remaining called "gospel oaks." There is one spot on the other side of the Thames known by the name of "Gospel Oak," and I have myself preached at Addlestone, in Surrey, under the far-spreading boughs of an ancient oak beneath which John Knox is said to have proclaimed the Gospel during his sojourn in England.[55] Many wild moors and lonely hillsides and secret spots in the forest have been consecrated in the same fashion, and traditions still linger over caves and dells and hilltops where, in old times, the bands of the faithful met to hear the Word of the Lord.

It would be an interesting task to prepare a volume of notable facts connected with open-air preaching or, better still, a consecutive history of it. I have no time for even a complete outline, but will simply ask you, Where would the Reformation have been if its great preachers had confined themselves to churches and cathedrals? How would the common people have become indoctrinated with the Gospel had it not been for those far-wandering evangelists, the missionaries, and those daring

---

55. One of my life's highlights was to open-air preach in London's famous Hyde Park. It was originally a place of public execution, but over the years evolved into a place designated for free public expression. Hundreds, if not thousands, pack that portion of the park each Sunday afternoon to listen to dozens of speakers climb soapboxes and speak on different subjects. It is easy to draw a crowd and is, therefore, a wonderful place to preach the Gospel.

innovators who found a pulpit on every heap of stones and an audience chamber in every open space near the abodes of men?

All through the Puritan times, there were gatherings in all sorts of out-of-the-way places, for fear of persecutors. "We took," said Archbishop Laud, in a letter dated Fulham, June, 1632, "another meeting of separatists in Newington Woods, in the very land where the king's stag was to be lodged, for his hunting next morning." A hollow or gravelpit on Hounslow Heath sometimes served as a meetingplace, and there is a dell near Hitchin where John Bunyan was wont to preach in perilous times. All over Scotland, the dells and vales and hillsides are full of covenanting memories to this day. You will not fail to meet with rock pulpits in which the stern fathers of the Presbyterian church thundered forth their denunciations of Erastianism and pleaded the claims of the King of Kings. Cargill and Cameron and their fellows found pleasant scenes for their brave ministries amid the mountains' lone rifts and ravines.

What the world would have been if there had not been preaching outside of walls and beneath a more glorious roof than these rafters of fir, I am sure I cannot guess. It was a brave day for England when Whitefield began field preaching. When Wesley stood and preached a sermon on his father's grave at Epworth because the parish priest would not allow him admission within the (so-called) sacred edifice, Mr. Wesley wrote, "I am well assured that I did far more good to my Lincolnshire parishioners by preaching three days on my father's tomb than I did by preaching three years in his pulpit."

Wesley wrote in his journal,

Saturday, 31 March, 1731. In the evening I reached Bristol, and met Mr. Whitefield there. I could scarce reconcile myself at first to this strange way of preaching in the fields, of which he gave me an example on Sunday; having been all my life (until very lately) so concerned with every point relating to decency and order, that I would have thought the saving of souls almost a sin, if it had not been done in a church."[56] Such were the feelings of a man who later became one of the greatest open-air preachers who ever lived!

Once it began, the fruitful agency of field-preaching was not allowed to cease. Amid jeering crowds and showers of rotten eggs and filth,[57] the immediate followers of the two great Methodists continued to storm village after village and town after town. They had various adventures, but their success was generally great. One often smiles when reading incidents in their labors. A string of pack horses was so driven to break up a congregation, and a fire engine was brought out and played over the throng to achieve the same purpose. Handbells, old kettles, trumpets, drums, and entire bands of music were engaged to drown the preachers' voices.[58]

In one case, the parish bull was let loose, and in others, dogs were set to fight. The preachers needed to have faces set like flints (see Isaiah 50:7), and so indeed they had. John Furz said,

> As soon as I began to preach, a man came straight forward and presented a gun at my face, swearing that he would blow my brains out if I spoke another word. However, I continued speaking, and he continued swearing, sometimes putting the muzzle of the gun to my mouth, sometimes against my ear. While we were singing the last hymn, he got behind me, fired the gun, and burned off part of my hair.

---

56. This at first seems a rather humorous attitude, but sadly, this is the mentality of many within the contemporary church. It would seem that the saving of souls should be confined to the use of soft music, an altar call and dimmed lights in a building many mistakenly call "the church."

57. The open-air preacher is at times subjected to great indignities. I have had many experiences that I cannot put in print and would not share in mixed company.

58. Such words are extremely comforting. I have been drowned out by church bells, guitars, drums, pianos, screaming females, megaphones, and a host of other sounds.

After this, my friends, we should never speak of petty interruptions or annoyances. The proximity of a firearm in the hands of a *"son of Belial"* (1 Samuel 25:17) is not very conducive to collected thought and clear utterance, but the experience of Furz was probably no worse than that of John Nelson, who coolly said,

> But when I was in the middle of my discourse, one at the outside of the congregation threw a stone, which cut me on the head. However, that made the people give greater attention, especially when they saw the blood run down my face,[59] so that all was quiet until I was done and was singing a hymn.

I have no time further to illustrate my subject by descriptions of the work of Christmas Evans and others in Wales, or of the Haldanes in Scotland, or even of Rowland Hill and his group in England. If you wish to pursue the subject, these names may serve as hints for discovering abundant material; and I may add to the list *The Life of Dr. Guthrie,* in which he recorded notable open-air assemblies at the time of the Disruption,[60] when as yet the Free Church had no places of worship built with human hands.

I must linger a moment over Robert Flockhart of Edinburgh, who, though a lesser light, was a constant one and a fit example to the bulk of Christ's street witnesses. Every evening, in all weathers and amid many persecutions, this brave man continued to speak in the street for forty-three years. Think of that, and never be discouraged. When he was tottering to the grave, the old soldier was still at his post. "Compassion to the souls of men drove me to the streets and lanes of my native city,"

---

59. I have found this to be true. I have been beaten up (by a woman) and have been able to keep speaking. Any sort of blood will gather a crowd, and is therefore well worth the pain. Stephen kept preaching right up until his promotion to Headquarters. (See Acts 7:58–59.) I don't advise seeking a fight, however, merely for the purpose of drawing a crowd.
60. The Disruption was a large split in the Church of Scotland in 1843.

he said, "to plead with sinners and persuade them to come to Jesus. The love of Christ constrained me."[61]

Neither the hostility of the police, nor the insults of the crowd could move him; he rebuked error in the plainest terms and preached salvation by grace with all his might. Edinburgh remembers him still. There is room for such in all our cities and towns and need for hundreds of his noble order in this huge nation of London—can I call it less?

No sort of defense is needed for preaching outdoors, but it would take a very strong argument to prove that a man who has never preached beyond the walls of his meetinghouse had done his duty. A defense is required rather for services within buildings rather than for worship outside of them. Apologies are certainly wanted for architects who pile up brick and stone into the skies when there is so much need for preaching rooms among poor sinners down below. Defense is greatly needed for forests of stone pillars, which prevent the preacher from being seen and his voice from being heard; for high-pitched Gothic roofs in which all sound is lost, and men are killed by being compelled to shout until they burst their blood vessels; and also for the willful creation of echoes by exposing hard, sound-refracting surfaces to satisfy the demands of art to the total overlooking of the comfort of both audience and speaker.

Surely also some decent excuse is badly wanted for those childish people who waste money by placing hobgoblins and monsters on the outside of their preaching houses, and must have other ridiculous statues stuck up, both inside and outside, to deface rather than to adorn their churches and chapels. But no defense whatever is needed for using the heavenly Father's vast audience chamber, which is in every way so well fitted for the proclamation of a Gospel so free, so full, so expansive, so sublime.

The great benefit of open-air preaching is that we get so many newcomers to hear the Gospel who otherwise would never hear it. The Gospel command is, "*Go ye into all the world, and preach the gospel to*

61. This is the attitude of a normal biblical Christian.

every creature" (Mark 16:15), but it is so little obeyed that one would imagine that it ran thus, "Go into your own place of worship and preach the Gospel to the few creatures who will come inside." The verse, "*Go out into the highways and hedges, and compel them to come in*" (Luke 14:23), although it constitutes part of a parable, is worthy of being taken very literally; doing so, its meaning will be carried out best.

We should actually go into the streets and lanes and highways, for there are lurkers in the hedges, tramps on the highways, streetwalkers, and lane-haunter, whom we will never reach unless we pursue them into their own domains. Sportsmen must not stop at home and wait for the birds to come and be shot at; neither must fishermen throw their nets inside their boats and hope to take many fish. Traders go to the markets; they follow their customers and go out after business if it will not come to them. And so must we. Some of our preachers are droning on and on to empty pews and musty hassocks while they might be conferring lasting benefit upon hundreds by quitting the old walls for a while and seeking living stones for Jesus.

I am quite sure, too, that if we could persuade our friends in the country to come out a good many times in the year and hold services in a meadow or in a shady grove or on the hillside or in a garden or on a common, it would be all the better for the usual hearers. The mere novelty of the place would freshen their interest and wake them up. The slight change of scene would have a wonderful effect upon the ones who are likely to sleep. See how mechanically they move into their usual place of worship, and how mechanically they go out again. They fall into their seats as if at last they had found a resting place, they rise to sing with an amazing effort, and then they drop down before you have time for the doxology at the close of the hymn because they did not notice it was coming.

What logs some regular hearers are! Many of them are asleep with their eyes open. After sitting a certain number of years in the same old spot, where the pews, pulpit, galleries, and all things are always the same—except that they get a little dirtier and dingier every week—where everybody occupies the same position forever and forevermore, and the minister's face, voice, and tone are much the same from January to December, you get to feel the holy quiet of the scene and listen to what is going on as though it were addressed to "the dull cold ear of death."

As a miller hears his wheels as though he did not hear them or a stoker scarcely notices the clatter of his engine after enduring it for a little time or as a dweller in London never notices the ceaseless grind of the traffic, so do many members of our congregations become insensible to the most earnest addresses and accept them as a matter of course. The preaching and the rest of it get to be so usual that they might as well not be given at all. Hence, a change of place might be useful; it might prevent monotony, shake up indifference, suggest thought, and, in a thousand ways, promote attention and give new hope of doing good. A great fire that would burn some of our chapels to the ground might not be the greatest calamity that has ever occurred if it only woke some of those people who rival the seven sleepers of Ephesus and will never be moved as long as the old house and the old pews hold together.

Besides, fresh air and plenty of it is a grand thing for every mortal man, woman, and child. I preached in Scotland twice on a Sabbath day at Blairmore, on a little height by the side of the sea, and after discoursing with all my might to large congregations, numbered in the thousands, I did not feel half as exhausted as I often am when addressing a few hundred in some horrible "black hole of Calcutta" called a chapel. I trace my freshness and freedom from lethargy at Blairmore to the fact that the windows could not be shut down by people afraid of drafts and that the roof was as high as the heavens are above the earth. My conviction is that a man could preach three or four times on a Sabbath outdoors with less fatigue than he would occasion with one discourse delivered in an impure atmosphere, heated and poisoned by human breath, and carefully preserved from every refreshing infusion of natural air.

I once preached a sermon in the open air in haying time during a violent storm of rain. The text was, *"He shall come down like rain upon the mown grass: as showers that water the earth"* (Psalm 72:6), and surely we had the blessing as well as the inconvenience. I was sufficiently wet, and my congregation must have been drenched, but they stood it out, and I never heard that anybody was the worse in health—though, I thank God, I have heard of souls who were brought to Jesus under that discourse. Once in a while, and under strong excitement, such things do no one any harm, but we are not to expect miracles, nor wantonly venture upon a course of procedure that might kill the sickly and lay the foundations of disease in the strong.

Do not try to preach against the wind, for it is an idle attempt. You may hurl your voice a short distance by an amazing effort, but you cannot be well heard even by the few. I do not often advise you to consider which way the wind blows, but on this occasion I urge you to do it or else you will labor in vain. Preach so that the wind carries your voice toward the people and does not blow it down your throat, or else you will have to eat your own words.[62]

There is no telling how far a man may be heard with the wind. In certain atmospheres and climates, as for instance in that of Palestine, persons might be heard for several miles; and single sentences of well-known speech may in England be recognized a long way off, but I should gravely doubt a man if he asserted that he understood a new sentence beyond the distance of a mile. Whitefield is reported to have been heard a mile, and I have been myself assured that I was heard for that distance, but I am somewhat skeptical. Half a mile is surely enough, even with the wind, but you must make sure of that to be heard at all.

Heroes of the Cross—here is a field for you more glorious than the Cid ever beheld. *"Who will bring me into the strong city? who will*

---

62. Take this advice to heart. In addition, do not preach by a fountain. When you begin speaking, it may sound like a babbling brook, but after some time preaching, your voice will strain and the brook will begin to sound like Niagara Falls. If you can, choose a place to speak that is away from music, cars, and machinery of any kind. Look for surrounding buildings that will help contain your voice.

lead me into Edom?" (Psalm 60:9; 108:10). Who will enable us to win these slums and dens for Jesus? Who can do it but the Lord? Soldiers of Christ who venture into these regions must expect a revival of the practices of the good old times as far as brickbats[63] are concerned—and I have known a flowerpot to fall "accidentally" from an upper window in a remarkably slanting direction. Still, if we are born to be drowned, we will not be killed by flowerpots.

Under such treatment it may be refreshing to read what Christopher Hopper wrote under similar conditions more than a hundred years ago.

> I did not much regard a little dirt, a few rotten eggs, the sound of a cow's horn, the noise of bells, or a few snowballs in their season; but sometimes I was saluted with blows, stones, bricks, and bludgeons. These I did not like well; they were not pleasing to flesh and blood. I sometimes lost a little skin, and once a little blood, which was drawn from my forehead with a sharp stone. I wore a patch for a few days and was not ashamed; I gloried in the Cross. And when my small sufferings abounded for the sake of Christ, my comfort abounded much more. I never was more happy in my own soul or blessed in my labors.

I am somewhat pleased when I occasionally hear of a brother being locked up by the police, for it does him good, and it does the people good also. It is a fine sight to see the minister of the Gospel marched off by the servant of the law! It excites sympathy for him, and the next step is sympathy for his message. Many who felt no interest in him before are eager to hear him when he is ordered to quit, and still more so when he is taken to the station. The vilest of mankind respect a man who gets into trouble in order to do them good; and if they see unfair opposition excited, they grow quite zealous in the man's defense.

As to style in preaching outdoors, we learned from Wesley that it should certainly differ from much of what prevails indoors: "Perhaps if

63. Bricks used as missiles to throw at someone.

a speaker were to acquire a style fully adapted to a street audience, he would be wise to bring it indoors with him. A great deal of sermonizing may be defined as saying nothing at extreme length; but outdoors verbosity is not admired. You must say something and have done with it and go on to say something more, or your hearers will let you know.... It is very unpleasant to find your congregation dispersing, but it is also a very plain suggestion that your ideas are also much dispersed."[64]

In the street, a man must keep himself lively, use many illustrations and anecdotes,[65] and sprinkle a quaint remark here and there. It will never do to dwell for a long time on a single point. Reasoning must be brief and clear. The discourse must not be labored or involved, and the second point must not depend upon the first, for the audience is a changing one.[66] Each point must be complete in itself.... Come to the point at once, and come there with all your might.

Short sentences of words and short passages of thought are needed for the outdoors. Long paragraphs and long arguments had better be reserved for other occasions. In quiet country crowds there is much force in an eloquent silence, now and then interjected; it gives people time to breathe, and also to reflect. Do not, however, attempt this in a London street; you must go ahead, or someone else may run off with your congregation. In a regular field sermon pauses are very effective and are useful in several ways, both to speaker and listeners, but to a passing company that is not inclined for anything like worship, a quick, short, sharp address is most appropriate.

---

64. In the following pages, Spurgeon quotes Wesley heavily. We've left in the major points to retain the flow of Spurgeon's message.
65. See *The Evidence Bible* (Bridge-Logos Publishers) for a wealth of quotes and anecdotes to use in preaching.
66. This is why you must train yourself to repeat the entire message regularly. Say, "This is what I am saying," and then repeat the essence of what you have just said. Open up the Law. Preach the fact of the Judgment, the reality of hell, the glory of the Cross, and the need for repentance and faith. Go back to crossing swords with your hearers; don't be embarrassed to repeat the message again and again. Some will be new to the crowd, and sinful hearts are hard of hearing, so it won't hurt them to hear it again. The great Puritan Richard Baxter said, "Screw the truth into men's minds."

In the streets a man must be intense from beginning to end, and for that very reason he must be condensed and concentrated in his thought and utterance. If you give your listeners chaff, they will cheerfully return it into your own bosom. Good measure, pressed down and running over will they mete out to you. (See Luke 6:38.) Shams and shows will have no mercy from a street gathering.

Have something to say, look them in the face, say what you mean, put it plainly, boldly, earnestly, courteously, and they will hear you. Never speak against time or for the sake of hearing your own voice, or you will obtain some information about your personal appearance or manner of oratory which will probably be more true than pleasing.

It will be very desirable to speak so as to be heard, but there is no use in incessant yelling. The best street preaching is not what is done at the top of your voice, for it is impossible to lay the proper emphasis upon key passages when you are shouting with all your might the entire time. When there are no hearers near you and people are standing on the other side of the road to listen, would it not be advisable to cross over and save a little of the strength that is wasted as you try to be heard?[67]

A quiet, penetrating, conversational style seems to be the most effective. Men do not yell when they are pleading in deepest earnestness; generally, at such times they have generally less wind and a little more rain: that is, less rant and a few more tears. You will weary everybody and wear out yourself if you go on and on and on in one monotonous shout. Be wise now, therefore, you who wish to succeed in declaring your Master's message among the multitude. Use your voices as common sense would dictate.[68]

---

67. Many times I have saved my voice by moving closer to my hearers. Sometimes they may come closer at your admonition, but it is often easier to say, "Let me come a little closer to save my voice."

68. Do not whisper or scream at your hearers. If you whisper, no one will hear, and there is therefore no purpose in preaching. Even if you do speak up without shouting, some may say that you are speaking too loud. If this happens, answer them in a normal quiet voice to illustrate why you are lifting up your volume. More than likely they will not be able to hear what your are saying to them, and your point is therefore made.

In a tract published by that excellent society "The Open-Air Mission," I notice the following:

QUALIFICATIONS FOR OPEN-AIR PREACHERS

1. A good voice.

2. Naturalness of manner.

3. Self-possession.

4. A good knowledge of Scripture and common things.

5. Ability to adapt himself to any congregation.

6. Good illustrative powers.

7. Zeal, prudence, and common sense.

8. A large, loving heart.

9. Sincere belief in all he says.

10. Entire dependence on the Holy Spirit for success.

11. A close walk with God by prayer.

12. A consistent walk before men by a holy life.

If any man has all these qualifications, the Queen had better make a bishop of him at once, yet none of these qualities can be dispensed of.

DEFINITE DIRECTIONS FOR OPEN-AIR PREACHING

Gawin Kirkham
The following chapter was taken from the book
The Open-Air Preacher's Handbook, written by Gawin
Kirkham, the secretary of The Open-Air Mission of London,
England. The book, published in 1890, is still relevant for
open-air preaching today.

We are told that "open-air preaching can be learned only by doing it." No doubt that is mostly correct, just as the art of swimming can be learned only in the water. But as the swimmer can learn more readily by a few plain directions, so the street preacher acquires his art more easily when aided by the experience of others. It is hoped, therefore, that the following hints will be found useful to those who desire to *"purchase to themselves a good degree, and great boldness in the faith which is in Christ Jesus"* (1 Timothy 3:13).

A Leader Is Essential. Someone should take charge of the meetings and choose the place, the hymns,[69] and the speakers. It is not necessary that he should be a practiced speaker or a good singer, but he should be able to arrange and control. It is desirable also to have a leader of the singing, so that the preachers do not strain their voices in attempting high notes. *"Let all things be done decently and in order"* (1 Corinthians 14:40).

The Choice of a Place. In villages, a preaching station is more easily chosen than in towns. The village street or the village green may be occupied, or a farmer will lend a field. But "field-preaching" is not so popular now as it was in the days of Wesley and Whitefield. As a rule, it is desirable to be so near the houses that those who do not care to come out may yet hear inside. But in towns, it is not desirable to select the busiest thoroughfares, unless it is on Sunday when there is less traffic. A side street just off the main street is best. Large open spaces are not suitable, unless the helpers are numerous and the singing attractive. A passage should always be kept clear on the sidewalk so that pedestrians do not need to go into the middle of the street.[70] *"Let every one of us please his neighbour for his good to edification"* (Romans 15:2).

The Order of Service. If the preacher is alone, like Jonah in Nineveh, he may begin by reading a chapter from his Bible, choosing a familiar and striking portion for this purpose. Or he may talk confidentially to two or three children until the curiosity of the grown-ups is awakened and they gather round. Or he may hand a few tracts to the strollers and idlers, encouraging them to come and hear. But if he has helpers, they had better sing first. Then a brief lesson may be read and a

---

69. Actual hymns may not be the best choice of music to draw a crowd today. They may actually keep the crowd away, as people associate hymns with stuffy church services.

70. This is an important point. For obvious reasons, the police will put an immediate stop to any preaching that blocks pedestrians and forces them to walk on the street. It is therefore wise to have a few bold helpers who are not afraid to say to the crowd, "Please keep the sidewalk free for pedestrians."

brief prayer offered.[71] But if the people are not likely to stay for reading and prayer, speaking may begin after the first hymn. The addresses, as a rule, should be brief—say, ten minutes or a quarter of an hour[72]—with singing between, and the meeting limited to an hour. But the wise leader will not confine himself to any definite order, as one of the charms of an open-air meeting is its freedom. *"Where the Spirit of the Lord is, there is liberty"* (2 Corinthians 3:17).

Open-air Pulpits. The curb is a sufficient elevation when speaking to a handful of people, but it is an immense advantage to stand on a stool, chair, or raised platform when speaking to an ordinary street crowd. The speaker can thus spare his voice and be better heard than when he is on the same level as the people. The common sense of street preachers is sadly lacking when they will not thus aid their voices by standing head and shoulders above the people.[73] Besides, this method is a scriptural one, for we read in the account of the great open-air meeting in *"the street that was before the water gate"* (Nehemiah 8:1, 3) in Jerusalem that *"Ezra the scribe stood upon a pulpit of wood, which they had made for the purpose"* (v. 4), and thus *"opened the book in the sight of all the people; (for he was above all the people)"* (v. 5). It is worthy of observation that that is the only place in the Bible where a *"pulpit"* is mentioned, so that the street preacher is fairly entitled to its use on the best authority. *"Jotham...stood in the top of mount Gerizim, and lifted up his voice, and cried"* (Judges 9:7).

The Value of Helpers. One of the most interesting sights to men and angels is a solitary preacher, crying like John the Baptist in the wilderness, *"Repent ye: for the kingdom of heaven is at hand"* (Matthew 3:2). But it is more to the preacher's comfort and the good of the work to have a band of helpers. Some can sing, while others can give tracts. They help to gather a crowd, to maintain order among the children, to keep the

---

71. I don't like openly praying in a public place. Prayer should be made before you reach your destination, so as not to alienate potential listeners. If you must pray where you are going to preach, make it discrete and be brief.

72. Rather, preach as long as you have something to say, a voice to say it with, and hearers to listen. You will be able to discern if people are listening or not.

73. See longer note at the end of this section.

pavement clear, and to cheer the preacher by their presence and their prayers. In commencing a meeting, instead of standing behind or at the side of the preacher, these helpers should face him, as if to form part of the audience, and encourage others to gather behind them. But, as a rule, they should not interfere with a disturber, as that is better done by the leader; nor should they be allowed to give tracts at the meeting while the service lasts. This latter course sadly distracts the attention of the hearers, though it is a very common proceeding on the part of kind and active helpers.[74] Christians should be encouraged to stand at open-air meetings, even if they cannot sing—ladies especially. *"Let your light so shine before men, that they may see your good works, and glorify your Father which is in heaven"* (Matthew 5:16).

The Art of Attraction. The preacher has first to secure and then to retain his hearers. Since "music has charms," good singing should be cultivated, and the singers should understand that harmony and sweetness are far more important than mere noise. Ladies render important service in street choirs. Solos, duets, trios, and quartets may occasionally be introduced, but the singing should be in harmony with the preaching and not merely a pretty performance to please the ear. It should be appropriate, lively, abundant, and entirely under the control of the leader of the meeting.

The distribution of hymn sheets is helpful in keeping a crowd together. A picture or diagram with lyrics is good for variety. Reed organs are the most common at open-air services, but a cornet is the most effective for leading the singing.[75] Prettily painted banners are pleasing to the eye, and when they have on them the name of the church or mission from which the workers come, they are useful in directing the people where to worship inside. A duplex lamp placed on a tripod is a great help in meetings after dark, though a street lamp may be made to

74. This point cannot be overemphasized. Make sure your helpers know when and when not to give out tracts. It isn't wise to distract someone from listening to the preaching by handing him a tract. Have helpers stand around the outskirts of the crowd and give tracts to those who aren't listening or who have been listening and are now leaving.
75. Today, of course, you can use more modern instruments, such as a guitar.

do duty where a special one cannot be had. But these arts of attraction must be in harmony with the apostle's rule: *"I am made all things to all men, that I might by all means save some"* (1 Corinthians 9:22).[76]

The Art of Preaching. Whatever means may be used to draw the people together, it will depend largely upon the preacher himself whether they are retained. Cold, formal, measured, precise preaching will not do. Nor will what may be called "a good sermon" indoors necessarily do outside. Life, fire, and energy are essential, just as our powder is essential to carry the shot. There is an indefinable style needed for open-air preaching that can be acquired only by practice.[77] The preacher's temptation is to rely too much upon impulse and surroundings, and so to neglect his studies. But if he is to be successful he must study; and his studies must include books, and men, and nature. The exhortation of Paul to Timothy is as important for the outdoor preacher as for the regular pastor—*"Give attendance to reading, to exhortation, to doctrine. Neglect not the gift that is in thee.... Meditate upon these things,...that thy profiting may appear to all"* (1 Timothy 4:13–15).

The Bible in the Street. The preacher's chief weapon must always be the Word of God, wielded by the power of the Holy Spirit. Yet the Bible must be sparingly used in the street. The lesson may be read from it; but in preaching, it is better to quote from it than to be perpetually giving chapter and verse, especially if this involves turning over the leaves to look for them. There is a powerful magnetism in the human eye; and the preacher's eye should rarely be taken off his hearers if he wishes to retain his hold of them. But the preacher who has the greatest knowledge of the Bible and the ability to quote appropriate texts correctly—other things being equal—will be the most successful. It is a good thing to set young preachers to read the lesson, as it encourages them afterward to speak. Those who would bless and save their fellow creatures must heed the Lord's commission to Ezekiel: *"And thou shalt speak my words unto them, whether they will hear, or whether they will forbear"* (Ezekiel 2:7).

76. See longer note at the end of this section.
77. See longer note at the end of this section.

Voice Culture. But while the Word of God is the preacher's chief weapon, the human voice is the medium by which that weapon reaches the people. How many books have been written on the art of speaking—and yet how few really effective speakers there are! The voice is soon injured in the open air unless it is used with care. Generally, the young preacher starts in too high a key and in too loud a tone. He forgets the oft-repeated advice "Begin low, speak slow. Aim higher, take fire."

Aware of this danger, John Wesley said to his preachers, "For the sake of Christ, don't scream." There is no doubt that the moderate and steady use of the voice outdoors strengthens it and also the chest of the speaker. Yet there are times when—owing to some condition of body, atmosphere, or both—the voice of the most practiced speaker fails. It is then the height of folly to continue using it. It should rest, and only by that process will it be regained. Or if it becomes a little husky by speaking, it may often be recovered by singing, taking care to sing the part that is easiest. Spurgeon has a valuable lecture, entitled "On the Voice," in the first volume of his *Lectures to My Students*. If preachers would take the trouble to enunciate their words more distinctly, they would speak with far less labor and with more effect. *"Lift up thy voice like a trumpet"* (Isaiah 58:1).

The Cultivation of Reverence. It is true that we do not go into the streets to worship, but to proclaim the Gospel; nevertheless, if we are to commend *"ourselves to every man's conscience in the sight of God"* (2 Corinthians 4:2), there must be reverence in this open-air temple, as much as in a consecrated building. This is best accomplished by realizing the Lord's presence. *"Lo, I am with you alway"* (Matthew 28:20). This realized presence prevents the spirit of trifling and levity, which are, alas, far too common at open-air assemblies, on the part of both the preacher and his helpers. It was this realized presence that produced such a marvelous effect at the meeting *"in the street that was before the water gate,"* as described in Nehemiah 8:6, when the people *"bowed their heads, and worshipped the* LORD *with their faces to the ground."*

There is another aid to reverence in the attitude of the preacher. How many preachers fail to mark 1 Corinthians 11:4: *"Every man praying or prophesying* [i.e., preaching], *having his head covered, dishonoureth his head."* This is a plain direction, which should be adhered to except in very severe weather, or by those who are liable to take cold easily. A further aid to reverence is the attitude in prayer. Happily it is the custom almost universally for the preacher and his helpers to uncover their heads during prayer, and this act is a sermon in itself. There are so many disturbing elements outdoors that the promoters should do all in their power to produce a becoming solemnity at street meetings. *"Let us exalt his name together"* (Psalm 34:3).

How to Deal with Interruptions. But with the best arrangements and the wisest proceedings, interruptions will occur. If the police interfere, it is more seemly to give way than to have a dispute by standing on our rights.[78] If a thoroughfare is blocked, the police may interfere by virtue of the authority vested in them; but even if they are wrong, it is better for the preacher to complain to their superiors than to contend with them in the presence of a crowd, since he represents the Gospel of peace. If a homeowner complains, however frivolous the objection, the police are bound to remove the preacher on such complaint being made. He cannot legally be arrested, but he may be summoned before a magistrate for resisting lawful authority. If a drunkard interferes, it is generally useless to argue with him. The police should protect the preacher by removing him; but sometimes a kindhearted helper may persuade him to walk away. If the interruption is by a Catholic or an infidel, it means discussion; and if the preacher begins a discussion, there is an end of

---

78. This is true. I know of an open-air preacher who has been arrested many times. This may be because of his attitude rather than anything else. I have found by experience that the police will respond favorably to you if you respect their authority.

the preaching.[79] Men who have studied these questions in all their bearings may discuss them, for truth has nothing to fear from error; but the ordinary preacher shows his wisdom by continuing his preaching and declining discussion. *"Behold, I send you forth as sheep in the midst of wolves: be ye therefore wise as serpents, and harmless as doves"* (Matthew 10:16).

"The Conclusion of the Whole Matter" (Ecclesiastes 12:13). As the object and end of preaching is the glory of God and the salvation of sinners, the methods that are most likely to bring about this end should be pursued. Prayer, preaching, and perseverance will work wonders by the blessing of God. If one plan fails, another should be tried. Young preachers should not be discouraged, for it may be some time before they can determine the question whether the Lord means them to be open-air preachers or not. They should be urgent in season and out of season, seeking to pluck brands out of the fire. Success is more likely to be attained by connecting the outdoor meeting with an indoor one.

---

79. Charles Spurgeon's "Preach Christ or nothing: don't dispute or discuss except with your eye on the Cross" is good advice. This doesn't mean that you shouldn't answer the questions; it means that you shouldn't be distracted from your object. When friends and I have been tag-preaching, we have often had to walk behind the preacher and tap him on the ankle to remind him that he was being distracted down an evolutionary rabbit trail. It was something each off us often needed. Evolution and other subjects may tickle the intellect, but they don't address the conscience. God's Law does. For further instruction on this subject, freely listen to "Hell's Best Kept Secret" and "How to Witness" on www.livingwaters.com.

NOTES

73. Here is another important point. If you are going to preach in the open air, elevate yourself. For eighteen months, I preached without any elevation and hardly attracted any listeners. As soon as I did it "soapbox" style, people stopped to listen. Their attitude was, "What has this guy got to say?" They had an excuse to stop. Also, elevation will give you protection. I was once almost beaten by an angry 6′ 6″ gentleman who kept fuming, "God is love!" We were eye to eye...while I was elevated. Hecklers will often be offended by the fact that you are elevated. They will say things like, "Why are you standing on that box? Do you think you are better than the rest of us!" I usually say that I'm on a box because I'm short, and then I will get off for a moment to make the point. If you aren't short, however, you may say you are elevated so that people at the back can hear your voice. Elevation will also give you added authority. Often hecklers will walk right up to you and ask questions quietly. This is an attempt to stifle the preaching, and it will work if you are not higher than your heckler. If they come too close to me, I talk over their heads and tell them to go back to the heckler's gallery. They actually obey me because they get the impression I am bigger than they are. As Mr. Kirkham goes on to point out, Ezra was elevated when he preached the Law. (See Nehemiah 8:4–5.) Jesus preached the greatest sermon ever on a mount (see Matthew 5–7), and Paul went up Mars' Hill to preach. (See Acts 17:22.) If you can't find a hilltop to preach from, use a soapbox or a stepladder. R. A. Torrey said, "Take your own position a little above the part of the audience nearest you, upon a curbstone, chair, platform, rise in the ground, or anything that will raise your head above others so that your voice will carry."

76. Our desire is for sinners to gather under the sound of the Gospel. If you don't have access to talented singers who are able to gather a crowd, there is perhaps another way to draw a crowd in. It is to give away money. Jesus informed us that there are two things in this world that people love: God or money. He told us that if they don't love God, they will instead love money. It will be their source of joy, their security, and a means of getting their attention. (Jesus often used money to get the attention of His hearers: He told stories about money, He asked people to show Him money, and He used money to make a point.)
Hold ten or twelve dollars in your hand, where they can be seen, and say, "I'm going to give away some money in a few minutes, so gather around. I will ask some simple questions. Get the answer correct, and you get the money!" Then ask those who are listening what they think is the greatest killer of drivers in the U.S. This stirs their curiosity. Some begin calling out "Alcohol!" or "Falling asleep at the wheel!" Tell them it's not these things, and repeat the question a few more times, saying that you will give a dollar to the person who gets the answer. Tell them that they will never guess what it is that kills more drivers than anything else in America. A few more shouts emit from the crowd. People are now waiting around for the answer. What is it that kills more drivers than anything else in the United States? What is it that could be the death of you and me? You won't believe this, but it is trees. Millions of them line our highways, waiting to kill a driver. When a tree is struck, it stays still, sending the driver into eternity. Then tell the crowd that you have another question for them. Ask what they think is the most common food on which people choke to death in U.S. restaurants. Over the next few minutes, go through the same scenario. People call out "Steak!" "Chicken bones!" Believe it or not, the answer is hard-boiled egg yoke. By now you have a crowd that is enjoying what is going on. Ask them what they think is the most dangerous job in America. Someone calls out "police officer." It's not. Someone else may name another dangerous profession like "firefighter." Say, "Good one...but wrong." Give a suggestion by saying, "Why doesn't someone say 'electrician'?" Someone takes the suggestion and says, "Electrician!" Say, "Sorry, it's not electrician." The most dangerous job in the

United States...is to be the president. Out of forty or so, four have been murdered while on the job, making the death rate ten percent. Then tell the crowd you have another question. "Does anyone in the crowd consider himself to be a 'good person'?" By now you will have noted who in the crowd has the self-confidence to speak out. Point to one or two and ask, "Sir, do you consider yourself to be a good person?" The Bible tells us that *most men will proclaim each his own goodness* (Proverbs 20:6), and he does. He smiles and says, "Yes, I do consider myself to be a good person." Ask him if he has ever told a lie. Has he stolen, lusted, blasphemed, and so on? That's when all heaven breaks loose. There is conviction of sin. Sinners hear the Gospel, and angels rejoice.

More Questions for Drawing Crowds:

+ Who wrote, "Ask not what your country can do for you. Ask what you can do for your country"? (President Kennedy's speechwriter)
+ What is the only fish that can blink with both eyes? (A shark)
+ Who was John Lennon's first girlfriend? (Thelma Pickles)
+ How long does it take the average person to fall asleep: 2 minutes, 7 minutes, or 4 hours? (7 minutes)
+ How long is a goldfish's memory span: 3 seconds, 3 minutes, or 3 hours? (3 seconds)
+ How many muscles does a cat have in each ear: 2, 32, or 426? (32)

If you have other Christians with you, have them form an audience and look as though they are listening to your preaching. This will encourage others to stop and listen. Tell the Christians never to stand with their backs to the preacher. I have seen open-air meetings when a fellow laborer is preaching for the first time, and what are the Christians doing? They are talking among themselves. Why, then, should anyone stop and listen if those in front of the speaker aren't even attentive? It is so easy to chat with friends when you've heard the Gospel a million times before. I have found myself doing it, but it is so disheartening for the preacher to speak to the backs of a crowd. Also, instruct Christians not to argue with hecklers. That will ruin an open-air meeting. I have seen an old lady hit a heckler with her umbrella and turn the crowd from listening to the Gospel to watching the fight she had just started. Who can blame them? Remember, the enemy will do everything he can to distract your listeners. Don't let him.

77. This is difficult to explain using the written word, but I will try. If you listened to me share the Gospel with one or two people, you would probably notice an obvious gentleness in my tone. However, if you listened to me preach in the open air, my tone might seem contentious and provocative. This is because if I preached the same way I speak, I would never hold a crowd. It is important in both cases that I be motivated by love, but if I don't keep the preaching "on the edge," I will lose my hearers in minutes—if not seconds. John Wesley put it this way: "In the streets a man must from beginning to end be intense, and for that very reason he must be condensed and concentrated in his thought and utterance." This "intense" preaching may be misunderstood by those who don't know why it's there. The problem is that when we read the Gospels, we don't see the passion involved in discourses. When Jesus spoke, there were those in the crowd who wanted to kill Him. They hated Him. People no doubt called out, accusing Him of blasphemy or asking Him questions. I am sure the atmosphere was electric, and such an atmosphere holds a crowd's attention. To become passive in the name of love and gentleness is to pull the plug on all evangelistic electricity. Beware, you may be accused of preaching without love. The accusations almost always come from those who have never preached in the open air. When speaking of open-air preaching, R. A. Torrey said, "Don't be soft. The crowd cannot and will not stand one of these nice, namby-pamby, sentimental sort of fellows in an open-air meeting. The temptation to throw a brick or a rotten apple at him is perfectly irresistible, and one can hardly blame the crowd."

ALLY IN THE HEART
OF THE ENEMY

Ray Comfort

One of the most memorable days in my life was when Kirk Cameron called me for the first time. He had listened to a tape called "Hell's Best Kept Secret."[80] He then visited our ministry, and over time we became the best of friends.

Again and again he would ask the question, "How can we get this teaching to the church? It is *so* important." I had been asking that same question for just under twenty years. So, in an effort to get it to the contemporary church, we combined ministries—he kindly loaned his "celebrity."

The power of a Hollywood name never ceases to amaze both of us. We often travel together, and many times a flight attendant will whisper, "Would you guys like to move up to first class?" I am quick to say "Yes!" and hold on to the coattails of Kirk's celebrity as we walk down the aisle of the plane.

---

80. See the book of the same name: *Hell's Best Kept Secret* (New Kensington, PA: Whitaker House, 1989, 2004).

But even greater things are happening than traveling first class—this teaching *is* getting to the church via "Way of the Master" seminars, books, CDs, tapes, and videos, and through our *Way of the Master* television program.[81]

Whenever doors open and thousands of people show up to our seminars, we both look at each other and think that this must be the hand of God.

We trust that as you have read through the sermons of the great men in this book, you have seen a thread of continuity. Each of these men of God used a key that God has given us, a key to bring sinners to the Savior. If by chance you have missed seeing this incredible key, this chapter encapsulates the teaching.

Have you ever thought, "There must be a key to reaching the lost"? Well, there is a key—and it's rusty through lack of use. The Bible does actually call it *"the key"* (Luke 11:52), and its purpose is to bring us to Christ, to unlock the door of the Savior (John 10:9). Jesus used it (Luke 10:26). So did Paul (Romans 3:19–20), Timothy (1 Timothy 1:8–11), and James (James 2:10). Stephen used it when he preached (Acts 7:53). Peter found that it was used to open the door to release three thousand imprisoned souls on the Day of Pentecost. *Yet much of the church still doesn't even know that it exists.* Not only is it biblical, but it can also be shown that the church has used it to unlock the doors of genuine revival many times throughout history. This key to revival is none other than the Law, as we shall see shortly.

Keys have a way of getting lost, and this key was no exception. Jesus said that the *"lawyers"* had *"taken away"* the key (Luke 11:52) and even refused to use it to let people enter into the kingdom of God. The Pharisees, unlike the lawyers, didn't take it away: Instead, they bent it out of shape so that it wouldn't do its work. (See Mark 7:8.) Jesus returned it to its true shape, just as the Scriptures prophesied that He would do. (See Isaiah 42:21.) Since then, Satan has tried to prejudice

81. See www.livingwaters.com.

the church against the key. He has maligned it, misused it, twisted it, and, of course, hidden it. He hates it because of the convicting work it does.

In Acts 28:23 the Bible tells us that Paul sought to persuade his hearers *"concerning Jesus, both out of the law of Moses, and out of the prophets."* Here we have two effective means of persuading the unsaved *"concerning Jesus."* Let's first look at how the prophets can help persuade sinners concerning Jesus. Fulfilled prophecy *proves* the inspiration of Scripture. The proclamations of the prophets present a powerful case for the inspiration of the Bible. Any skeptic who reads the prophetic words of Isaiah, Ezekiel, Joel, or any other prophet and then reads the account of Jesus' life recorded in the Gospels cannot help but realize that the Bible is no ordinary book.

The other means by which Paul persuaded sinners concerning Jesus was *"out of the law of Moses."* The Bible tells us that the Law of Moses is good if it is used lawfully (1 Timothy 1:8). It was given by God as a *"schoolmaster"* to bring us to Christ (Galatians 3:24). Paul wrote that he *"had not known sin, but by the law"* (Romans 7:7). From these Scriptures and others, we can conclude that the Law of God (the Ten Commandments) is *"the key of knowledge"* that Jesus spoke of in Luke 11:52. He was speaking to *"lawyers"*—those who should have been teaching God's Law so that sinners would receive the *"knowledge of sin"* (Romans 3:20) and thus recognize their need for the Savior. While prophecy speaks to the *intellect* of a sinner, the Law speaks to his *conscience.* Prophecy produces *faith* in the truth of the Word of God while the Law brings *knowledge* of sin in to the hearts of sinners.

The Law is the God-given "key" to unlock the door of salvation. Charles Spurgeon said, "I do not believe that any man can preach the Gospel who does not preach the Law. The Law is the needle, and you cannot draw the silken thread of the Gospel through a man's heart unless you first send the needle of the Law to make way for it."

Sadly, the moment that most people in the contemporary church hear the word "Law," they immediately think of "legalism." While it is true that many use the Law unlawfully and twist it into a legalistic religion, that should not prohibit us from using the Law evangelistically—to reach the lost. That why God gave it, "*for sinners*" (1 Timothy 1:9).

If you study how Jesus evangelized in Mark 10:17–21, you will notice how different His approach was from that of many modern evangelists. An earnest young man ran to Jesus, knelt down in humility, called Jesus "*good*" (v. 17), and then asked how he could obtain eternal life. Jesus didn't immediately preach the Cross or speak of God's endless love to this potential convert. Instead, He corrected the man's understanding of the word "*good.*" Then He took the man through the Ten Commandments (the moral Law) to show him what sin was. We need to imitate the way of the Master when it comes to dealing with the unsaved. Conviction must always precede conversion, and this can come only by knowledge and the Law.

So how can we practically implement this incredible tool that Charles Spurgeon called "our most powerful weapon"?

This is how: I'm sitting in a plane next to a man. I smile and say, "Hi, how are you doing? Do you have one of these? It's a gospel tract." He says he did not receive one, and I give him one, asking, "Would you consider yourself to be a good person?" When he says, "Yes, I do," I take him through the Ten Commandments to show him God's standard of goodness, beginning with "Have you ever told a lie?" When he says that he has, I ask him if he has ever stolen anything. Then I say that Jesus said, "Whoever looks upon a woman to lust after her has committed adultery already with her in his heart." When he admits that he has also lusted, I gently say, "By your own admission you are a lying, thieving adulterer at heart…and we've looked at only three of the Ten Commandments." I shut him up under the Law, and then bring the mercy of the Cross, repentance, and faith.

I'm sitting in a plane next to a Roman Catholic. There are millions of Catholics and Protestants who have never been born again and, therefore, need to hear the Gospel. So I smile and say, "Hi, how are you doing? Do you have one of these? It's a gospel tract." He answers, "I'm a Roman Catholic." At this point, I needn't panic, thinking that I am going to have to talk about papal infallibility, the confessional, praying to the saints, purgatory, transubstantiation, or the role of the Virgin Mary. I simply ask him, "Would you consider yourself to be a good person?" When he answers, "Yes, I do," I take him through the Ten Commandments to show him God's standard of goodness, beginning with "Have you ever told a lie?"

I'm sitting in a plane next to a homosexual. I smile and say, "Hi, how are you doing? Do you have one of these? It's a gospel tract." We talk for a while, and I find out he's gay. At this point, I needn't panic, thinking that I am going to have to talk about his sexual orientation. I simply ask him, "Would you consider yourself to be a good person?" When he answers, "Yes, I do," I take him through the Ten Commandments to show him God's standard of goodness, beginning with "Have you ever told a lie?"

I'm sitting in a plane next to an intellectual. I smile and say, "Hi, how are you doing? Do you have one of these? It's a gospel tract." He answers, "I'm an evolutionist, and I lean strongly toward the controversial spontaneous regeneration and the quantum embryonic theory of cosmological physics." I'm not intimidated. I simply answer with, "Would you consider yourself to be a good person?" When he says, "Yes, I do," I take him through the Ten Commandments to show him God's standard of goodness, beginning with "Have you ever told a lie?"

You may have noticed a repetition. This is for the purpose of making an incredibly important point: It is essential in evangelism that we circumnavigate the human intellect and speak directly to the conscience. The specific words I use are not important, nor is there a "magic formula" for conversion that I must memorize. The point is simply to bring the knowledge of sin to an unrepentant sinner by using the moral Law of God as a schoolmaster to lead him to Christ.

Again, this is what Jesus did (see Mark 10:17–21); it is the way of the Master. You see, the human mind is at war with God and not subject to the Law of God (Romans 8:7). For me to be effective, I have to find ground upon which there is agreement about the Law so that I can *reason* with the sinner about sin, righteousness, and judgment to come. This place of common ground is the conscience: "*Which show the work of the law written in their hearts, their conscience also bearing witness*" (Romans 2:15).

The sinful human mind is bent on arguing with the Law, but the conscience will agree with it. Use the Law of God to speak directly to the conscience. The human understanding is *"darkened"* (Ephesians 4:18), but the conscience is the area where God has given light to every man.

The word *con-science* means "with knowledge." The conscience is the bold headline that warns of sin. No man can say he doesn't know that it's wrong to murder or commit adultery; that knowledge is written in large print on his heart. In the Scriptures, however, we see the true nature of sin—that God requires truth even in the inward parts (Psalm 51:6). The fine print reveals that lust is adultery of the heart and hatred is murder of the heart. When we face the Law, we are all convicted.

Some people seem to have no conscience. In truth, they have a "*seared*" conscience (see 1 Timothy 4:2), one that has become so hardened that it has lost its ability to fully function. A correct use of the Law, however, will resurrect it. When you speak directly to the conscience of a hardened sinner by saying, "You *know* that it's wrong to steal, to lie, to commit adultery," the conscience affirms the truth of the Commandment.

Often, we complicate witnessing by bringing up issues that are irrelevant to the subject of salvation. This confines us to the intellect (the place of argument), rather than the conscience (the place of the knowledge of sin).

Martin Luther said,

> As long as a person is not a murderer, adulterer, thief, he would swear that he is righteous. How is God going to humble such a person except by the Law? The Law is the hammer of death, the thunder of hell, and the thunder of God's wrath to bring down the proud and shameless hypocrites. When the Law was instituted on Mount Sinai, it was accompanied by lightning, by storms, by the sounds of trumpets, to tear to pieces that monster called self-righteousness. As long as a person thinks he is right, he is going to be incomprehensibly proud and presumptuous. He is going to hate God, despise His grace and mercy, and ignore the promises in Christ. The Gospel of free forgiveness of sins though Christ will never appeal to the self-righteous. This monster of self-righteousness, this stiff-necked beast, needs an axe. And that is what the Law is, a big axe. Accordingly, the proper use and function of the Law is to threaten until the conscience is scared stiff.

What place, then, do apologetics have? They should have the same purpose as a worm does on a hook. They are merely bait for the intellect. They attract the fish but do not catch them. Never let the fish spend too long nibbling on the bait or else he'll escape before you can hook him. Learn to quickly pull the hook of the Law into the human heart. Discover how to quickly move from intellect to conscience, just as Jesus did.

This is why we compiled *The Evidence Bible* (Bridge-Logos Publishers). We wanted to put tools into your hands. It has been commended by Josh McDowell, Dr. D. James Kennedy, and Franklin Graham. (It was also a finalist in the 2002 Gold Medallion Book

Awards.) It contains more than two decades worth of research, and not only teaches principles such as those discussed in this chapter, but also provides other incredible pieces of information, such as how to show the absurdity of evolution, how to share your faith with your family or at your workplace, how to make an atheist "backslide," and how to prove the authenticity of the Bible through prophecy.

Many Christians don't realize that the Bible is full of eye-opening scientific and medical facts, nor are they aware of fascinating and faith-building quotes from Albert Einstein, Sir Isaac Newton, Louis Pasteur, Stephen Hawking, and many other well-known scientists. One great highlight of the publication is that it contains one hundred of the most commonly asked questions of the Christian faith, as well as the combined evangelistic wisdom of Charles Spurgeon, D. L. Moody, John Wesley, Charles Finney, George Whitefield, Josh McDowell, Billy Graham, Dr. Bill Bright, John MacArthur, R. C. Sproul, and many others.

I would like to end this chapter with an e-mail we received from Darrel L. Rundus II, Maui, Hawaii. Through a series of strange circumstances, he was assured that God wanted him to travel five thousand miles to attend his grandmother's funeral:

> The only reason I was taking the flight was due to an act of God; I knew that there had to be more to it than just attending my grandma's funeral. I prayed to thank God for His obvious guidance and for making my paths straight and decisions easy, and I kept thinking about what the Holy Spirit had put in my heart a few days earlier (Luke 9:60). Suddenly, it came to me. I wasn't going to Kansas City just to attend the funeral; I needed to be prepared to preach the Word on the airplane and/ or in Kansas City. Maybe even at the funeral to family whom I hadn't seen in years? I love it when God gives me a captive audience to preach the Gospel, so, when I packed for my flight the

night before, I made sure that my laptop bag was stuffed with Christian tracts, pennies, New Testaments, and some "Magic Flyer" butterflies.

While in prayer with my wife and kids before getting out of the van to check in for my flight, the Holy Spirit showed me a vision. I was witnessing to a man who was over fifty and a doctor of some kind. So, as you might imagine, I was a little confused and relieved when I ended up sitting next to a thirteen-year-old girl and her brother once we boarded the plane.

About an hour after the plane took off, you'll never guess what happened. Amazingly the girl and her father decided to change seats, and who was sitting next to me? You guessed it—a gentleman who was around fifty years old and was, of all things, a veterinarian. Knowing this was a divine appointment, I started talking with this gentleman about natural things. You know, "What brought you to Maui?" and "Did you have a good time?" I asked him, "What kind of work do you do?" The answer only confirmed my vision and compelled me to take the next step.

After paying him a few compliments regarding his family, I asked, "Would you consider yourself a good person?" He, as most will do, proclaimed his own righteousness and said, "Yes." I then asked him if he thought he had kept the Ten Commandments, and he said he didn't know because he wasn't sure what all of them were. So with that, I immediately pulled a Ten Commandment penny from my pocket and said, "Well, let's go over a few of them and see if you've kept them, okay?" I handed him the penny and proceeded to ask if he'd ever told a lie, ever stolen, or ever looked with lust. He said yes to all three. When I started to move on to ask him if he thought he'd be innocent or guilty on Judgment Day, he said, "Wait, I'd like to go over the rest of the Commandments to see what they are and how I've done."

Amazed but not wanting to discourage his interest, I gladly obliged him. I knew that the more he looked into the mirror of God's Law, the more convicted he'd become. "Have you always put God first?" I asked. "Have you ever made up a god in your mind that wasn't biblical in order to suit your own lifestyle?" "Have you ever put money before God?" "Have you ever used the Lord's name in vain?" I went on until I had gone over all of them, and he had pleaded guilty on all ten counts (based on the standards set by Jesus). In fact, the Law of God did such a good job plowing his heart for the seed of the Gospel that, I must admit, due to the contrition on his face, before I shared the "Good News" with him, I first consoled him. I asked him not to feel too condemned by my pointing out his sins, for I, too, am guilty on all ten counts.

I then shared the Good News about God loving us so much that He was willing to become a man in Jesus and sacrifice Himself for the sins of the world. I shared the Resurrection, and redemption by the blood of Christ. The really amazing thing was that, after I had preached the Gospel to him, he admitted that he had been a member of the Episcopal Church for many years but had never truly realized why he needed Jesus. Here was a good, church-going father of two great kids who, up until that plane ride, never truly saw the need for God's forgiveness for his sins. He went to church because he thought that was the best environment for his kids and wanted to do the right thing. The sad fact was, he didn't go to church to worship God or because he was trying to obey the Commandments. To him, it was more of a social thing than an "I love God" thing. Most of all, he never had a repentant heart until the night he looked long and hard into the mirror of God's Law. I'll never forget the convicted look on his face as I shared all Ten Commandments with him.

I chuckle to myself when thinking about the shocked look that must have been on my face when he asked me to go over the other seven Commandments with him! After I was done, there was no need for me to ask if he saw the need for God's forgiveness, since it was written all over his face. I will also never forget the peace and understanding on his face when I shared the Gospel with him. It was as if he finally saw the significance of the sacrifice Jesus made on the cross. It was as if he saw God's plan unfolded before his eyes, and the life, death, and resurrection of Jesus finally made sense to him. The Law of God completely bypassed his intellect and cut straight through to his conscience. It was as if Jesus Himself had pierced this man's heart with the sword of His Spirit.

Mostly, I'll never forget the light in his eyes and the love in his heart after he prayed to commit his life to Christ right there on the airplane, in the middle of the night. I knew he really felt it due to the contrition, weeping, brokenness, and enlightenment. I knew Christ entered his heart that night because of the unbelievable energy in his words and in his face as we spoke all night about Christ until we landed in Dallas the next morning.

—Darrel L. Rundus II, Maui, Hawaii

APPENDIX

For years, I have complained that there is nowhere to open-air preach in the U.S. People are either in cars, at the movies, attending sporting events, at shopping malls, or doing something on other private property. For over four years, I gave out tracts to a long line of people who were waiting each morning outside the courtroom opposite our ministry, because this was the only place I could reach a crowd on public property.

One day, however, I was challenged to preach to them. I decided to do it on a particular morning, but during the night I got a tickle in my throat and decided not to preach.

Shortly after that, an earthquake struck the Los Angeles area. It wasn't a gentle rolling motion, but rather a powerful jolt, that woke both Sue and me from deep sleep. It was as if a giant baseball bat had struck our house. It is amazing how an earthquake can help get priorities straightened; I vowed then and there to carry out the preaching I had committed to do.

The next day, I nervously stood in front of the crowd. "Good morning," I said. "My name is Ray. I'm a local pastor, and I'm going to speak to you for a few moments. What I am going to say may offend some of you, but I would like you to think about the fact that over one hundred Americans recently died in Iraq so that you and I could have the liberty of free speech in this country. Please bear that in mind as I speak.

"You are here because you have allegedly violated civil law. The Bible alleges that each of us have violated God's Law—the Ten Commandments. So I would like to put you on the stand, cross-examine you for a moment under the light of that Law, and then let you make the call as to whether you are innocent or guilty."

I then went through the Law and the reality of hell. I explained that confessing their sins to God on Judgment Day wouldn't help them. I told them that it was like saying to the judge they were about to face, "Judge, I confess I committed the crime. I'm sorry." The judge would probably say, "So, you are admitting your guilt. Then you should be sorry and will have no problem paying up, for you've broken the law."

I explained that they needed someone to pay their fine. I told them about the Cross, repentance, and faith in Jesus. I closed by telling them that my ministry partner is Kirk Cameron, whom they might remember from the sitcom "Growing Pains." "We would like to give you a book about his latest movie that will help you in your walk with God," I said. "Please take it as I walk past you." They all seemed to be listening, no one was offended, and all the books that I had were taken.

The next day, my son-in-law and I did the same thing, and we have been doing it ever since. Each day there is a fresh crowd—different people from all walks of life—with as many as one hundred people some mornings. I couldn't have asked for a better opportunity, and it was less than fifty yards from my doorstep! These folks are waiting to go to court, they are no doubt praying for mercy, and they can't get out of line because they will lose their place. We have a member of our team walk along the line, totally independent of us, advising them that they would need to turn cell phones and pagers off before they went inside and giving out tracts that we had especially designed and printed for the courts. They are called "Your Day in Court" and speak of how the person should conduct himself or herself in the courtroom. They then gently lead into the Gospel.

One day, an angry gentleman called out, "I'm going to exercise my First Amendment rights! Who the @!!$! are you!!!" I said, "My name is Ray..." and was about to "stir" him a little, as I had done for years when I found a potential heckler. Then I realized that I already had a crowd and didn't need to do so. He then mumbled, "I'm gonna call the police!" He didn't say a word after that. I guess he realized that he wasn't in a good position to call the law because he was on his way to court for violating the law himself.

As I walked passed him offering books to the line of people, I thought that I might get punched. He didn't even look up at me as I walked past, however. He was too busy reading the literature he had just been given...about his day in court.

ABOUT THE AUTHORS

Ray Comfort cohosts the award-winning TV program, *The Way of the Master*, airing in 190 countries. His YouTube channel, Living Waters, has more than 160 million views and more than 866,000 subscribers.

Ray is the CEO of LivingWaters.com and is the author of more than 100 books, including the best-seller *Hell's Best Kept Secret*, which has been called one of the most insightful books published on the subject of evangelism.

A native New Zealander, Ray began his ministry with a burden for his lost friends. After attending the funeral of a fifth friend who had died from a drug overdose, Ray published an eight-page pamphlet called "My Friends Are Dying." The pamphlet was later expanded to a paperback book, and Ray began sharing with youth about the ultimate answer to the drug problem—Jesus Christ.

Ray founded Living Waters to equip Christians of every denomination to reach out to the lost with a radically different method of evangelism that is powerful, effective, and non-intimidating. Believers learn how to witness the way Jesus did—by moving out of the realm of argument into the realm of the sinner's conscience, his place of knowledge of right and wrong. This principle is not only biblical, but it was also the powerful catalyst that made the ministries of Charles Spurgeon, John Wesley, George Whitefield, and other preachers so effective.

Ray lives with his wife Sue and three grown children in Southern California.

———

Kirk Cameron has been a part of the national landscape since starring as "Mike Seaver" in the 1980s hit sitcom, *Growing Pains*. Since then, he's appeared in dozens of television and movie productions, including the *Left Behind* series, *Monumental*, *Connect*, and *Fireproof*, the marriage-centered film that became the top grossing inspirational movie of 2008.

Kirk has been featured on the *Today* show, *Fox News*, *The Ben Shapiro Show*, and CNN. In 2016, he hosted Revive Us, a national family meeting urging the family of faith to return to the principles that will bring blessing and protection to America. He recently hosted the four-hour TV special *Think. Pray. Vote.*

Kirk is currently producing a new inspirational film about adoption and the value of preborn life. He and his wife, Chelsea, met on the set of *Growing Pains* and have been married for twenty-nine years. Together, they have six children and host an all-expenses-paid summer camp for terminally ill children and their families called Camp Firefly.

Welcome to Our House!

We Have a Special Gift for You

It is our privilege and pleasure to share in your love of Christian books. We are committed to bringing you authors and books that feed, challenge, and enrich your faith.

To show our appreciation, we invite you to sign up to receive a specially selected **Reader Appreciation Gift**, with our compliments. Just go to the Web address at the bottom of this page.

God bless you as you seek a deeper walk with Him!

WE HAVE A GIFT FOR YOU. VISIT:

whpub.me/nonfictionthx

WHITAKER
HOUSE